Camillo B. conte di Cavour

Thoughts on Ireland

Its present and its future. By the late Count Cavour. Tr. by W.B. Hodgson,

LL. D

Camillo B. conte di Cavour

Thoughts on Ireland
Its present and its future. By the late Count Cavour. Tr. by W.B. Hodgson, LL. D

ISBN/EAN: 9783337322397

Printed in Europe, USA, Canada, Australia, Japan

Cover: Foto ©Thomas Meinert / pixelio.de

More available books at **www.hansebooks.com**

THOUGHTS

ON

IRELAND:

ITS PRESENT AND ITS FUTURE.

BY THE LATE

COUNT CAVOUR.

TRANSLATED BY

W. B. HODGSON, LL.D.

LONDON:
TRÜBNER & CO., PATERNOSTER ROW.
MANCHESTER: A. IRELAND & CO., PALL MALL.

1868.

TO

THE RIGHT HONOURABLE

WILLIAM EWART GLADSTONE, M.P.,

IN THE FIRM BELIEF THAT

HIS MOMENTARY DEFEAT HERALDS HIS LASTING TRIUMPH,

𝕮𝖍𝖎𝖘 𝖁𝖔𝖑𝖚𝖒𝖊

IS RESPECTFULLY INSCRIBED

(WITHOUT PERMISSION)

BY

THE TRANSLATOR.

24th November, 1868.

" Ireland is now suffering under a circle of evils, producing and repro-
ducing each other :—want of capital produces want of employment, turbulence, and misery ; turbulence and misery, insecurity ; insecurity prevents
the introduction of capital, and so on. Until this circle is broken the evil
must continue, and probably augment."—*Report, in* 1836, *on the State of the
Poor in Ireland, by Geo. Nicholls, Esq.*, p. 20.

" In virtue of the long unsettlement of Ireland and her special claims
to consideration, she is affording a clear field for the discussion of political,
ecclesiastical, and social questions which the English nation, satisfied with
an early and limited progress, will not suffer to be mooted directly in
respect to itself. An Irish famine repealed the Corn Laws. Irish outrage
gave to the empire the benefit of a regularly organised police. The des-
perate state of Irish property led to the passing of an Encumbered Estates
Act. Ireland has introduced the system of mixed education. In Ireland,
the relations between landlord and tenant have been first made the subject
of discussion, with some prospect of an equitable solution. In Ireland was
promulgated the potent aphorism, 'Property has its duties as well as its
rights.' In Ireland, where the members of the dominant Church are in a
small and hopeless minority, and the Establishment is clearly a political
evil, the great question of Church and State will probably be first raised
with effect, and receive its most rational solution."—*Goldwin Smith* : *Irish
History and Irish Character.* 2nd Ed., 1862, p. 197.

PREFACE.

IN January and February, 1844, at a time when freedom of the press did not exist in Piedmont, there appeared in the *Bibliothèque Universelle de Genève* (Nouvelle Serie, Tom. 49,) the following article on "IRELAND, ITS PRESENT AND ITS FUTURE," by the late Count Cavour. In 1855, it was reprinted in a collection of the "Politico-Economical Works of Count Camille Benso di Cavour," published at Coni, and little known beyond, or even within, the bounds of Italy. It was written when the Repeal agitation in Ireland was at its height. On the 10th of September, 1843, at a great Repeal meeting, O'Connell promised he would have his Protection Society of three hundred sitting before Christmas. "I hope," he said, "to be able to give you, as a New Year's Gift, a parliament in College Green." On the 7th of October, within a week after the "monster meeting" at Mullaghmast, the Irish government issued a proclamation prohibiting a great Repeal meeting which was appointed for the following day at Clontarf, three miles from Dublin, at which persons on horseback were to have paraded as

the "Repeal Cavalry." All similar meetings were, at
the same time, declared illegal. In obedience to a proclamation issued thereupon by O'Connell, the meeting
was not held, and the day passed quietly. On the 14th
of October, O'Connell, John O'Connell, and several other
leading Repealers, were arrested on a charge of con-
spiracy, sedition, and unlawfully conspiring, but were held
to bail. The proceedings began on the 2nd of November,
the first day of term; but it was not till the 12th of
February, 1844, that the jury returned their verdict.
The issue is well known. On the 24th of May, the Irish
judges, having refused the motion for a new trial, sen-
tenced O'Connell to imprisonment for twelve months,
with a fine of £2,000, and bound him in his own recog-
nizance in the sum of £5,000, and two sureties of £2,500,
to keep the peace for seven years. On the 2nd of July,
the writs of error, in which O'Connell and his associates
in the State trials were plaintiffs, came before the House
of Lords; and, on the 4th of September, the law-lords
decided that the judgment of the court below ought to be
reversed. It was, then, while the case was still pending in
the Irish court, that Cavour's Essay appeared. If I do
not err, all that has occurred since that time tends to
increase, much rather than to diminish, the interest and
the value of the great Italian statesman's estimate of Irish
history, condition, and prospects. The failure of his

expectations, in so far as they have failed, is not less instructive than their fulfilment, in so far as they have been fulfilled. O'Connell's agitation for Repeal, indeed, collapsed, as Cavour predicted, and the state of Ireland has, in some degree, improved. But had Cavour lived till now, great must have been his disappointment that, in spite of the operation of the Encumbered Estates Act, passed in 1849,*—in spite of a vast amount of emigration,—in spite of the National School system,—in spite of all legislative measures,—Irish discontent has, after another quarter of a century,·burst forth in armed Fenianism;—the Habeas Corpus Act has been again for a long time suspended;—the great question of Ireland is still the hinge on which turns the fate of British ministries; and the problems of Irish land and Irish church still clamour for solution. Ireland is still, and will, too probably, long continue to be, the field on which the battle of English interests and English parties must be fought. A Protestant Church must, it seems, be maintained in Catholic Ireland lest a more and more doubtfully Protestant Church in England should be endangered; and the system of

---

* The number of Parliamentary titles registered in Ireland under the Record of Title (Landed Estates Court) Act, up to the 1st of August, 1867, was 200; and the value of the estates held thereunder is £564,049. 7s. 4d.—*Pall Mall Gazette*, 16th Sept., 1867.

National Schools in Ireland must, it seems, be subverted,
in order that the Denominational System of Education
in England may be maintained. In both cases, Commis-
sions have been appointed with the hope, in the former
case, that the institution may, with modifications, be in
principle preserved; in the latter, that the institution may
be, in principle, destroyed. The relation between landlord
and tenant, again, must not be touched in Ireland, lest a
precedent dangerous to England should be established.
Out of this terrible complication only a very wise, or a
very presumptuous man can attempt to trace any path of
speedy issue.   Though, of late, events have marched
rapidly, and though a crisis has almost suddenly come
upon us, the immediate prospect is by no means bright.
Liberal majorities, indeed, have, on the whole, declared
themselves in favour of equality against privilege, of
religion against sect, of right against the ascendancy of
party or of creed. Victory seems to smile on the banner
bearing the device *"Fiat Justitia, Ruat Ecclesia;"*—
but the strife will be hard and painful, whether it be
long or short. Mr. Disraeli, in view of an early retirement from the ministerial craft, and baffled in his ill-
disguised and worse denied overtures for an alliance with
Ultramontanism, has gone into partnership with Mr.
Murphy, in the business of "No POPERY" agitation;
and recent acts of mob-violence show that the demons

of theological rancour and national antipathy can too easily be evoked among the. ignorant and passionate masses of our people. Whatever the immediate issue, this appeal to too prevalent prejudice and animosity, this revival of passions which have disgraced and ensanguined the past, cannot fail to be a danger and a difficulty, and must be followed by a long train of evils. Let me hope that this voice from the grave of Cavour may be heard not without benefit on both sides of the channel. His impartial and generous sympathy with both England and Ireland, his strongly expressed and calmly reasoned conviction that, while the two countries cannot be, and ought not to be, separated, each country ought to be, and will yet be, a blessing to the other,— may, in some measure, urge Englishmen to persevere in the difficult task of conciliating Ireland (so long oppressed and so sadly alienated),—and encourage Irishmen to hope more, to hate less, and to join earnestly with what best deserves the name of England, in the effort to remove the political and social evils from which Ireland suffers, pre-eminently, but not alone.

W. B. H.

24th November, 1868.

THOUGHTS ON THE PRESENT STATE, AND ON THE FUTURE, OF IRELAND.

THE present singular condition of Ireland has excited the attention of all in Europe who are interested in politics. There is, perhaps, no one who has not put to himself the question, with a full sense of its difficulty,— What may be the issue of a movement which one extraordinary man has been able to institute, and which he guides with skill so marvellous? The European journals, faithful interpreters of the general thought, make Ireland one of the habitual themes of their discussions. Usually brief on the affairs of England, they open their columns to reports of the smallest "meetings" at which repeal of the Union is demanded, and they regularly inform us of the most minute details of the great law-case in which O'Connell and his associates are at this hour engaged. What means this general excitement? Can it announce the approach of one of those great political crises which so profoundly modify the social being of nations? Does this crisis threaten with a violent catastrophe the ancient edifice of the British constitution, which ages have respected, and which European revolutions, far from shaking, have rather consolidated? From the hopes, the ill-concealed joy of certain journals, of certain political parties, when they speak of Ireland, one might be tempted

B

to this belief. The enemies of England on the continent, and their number is unhappily very considerable, imagine that the day of vengeance draws near; her friends hesitate, and feel their faith shaken in that constitution which, more than any other in the world, they used to believe to be safe from political shocks.

Public opinion on the continent is not, it must be said, generally favourable to England. Extreme parties, opposed in all besides, agree in their violent hatred of that country. Moderate parties love it in theory; but in reality they feel towards it little instinctive sympathy. Only a few isolated men, superior to the passions of the crowd and to the popular instincts, cherish towards England the esteem and interest which may well be inspired by one of the greatest nations that have done honour to humanity: a nation which has powerfully contributed to the material and moral development of the world, and whose civilising mission is yet far from being accomplished. The masses are everywhere hostile to it.

Let it not be thought that in France only does this sentiment prevail. In that country it is manifested in a more lively and noisy fashion; but, in truth, it is common to all the nations of Europe. From St. Petersburg to Madrid, in Germany as in Italy, the enemies of progress, and the partisans of political revolutions alike regard England as their most formidable foe. The former accuse it of being the centre in which all revolutions are planned, the assured refuge, the citadel, so to speak, of propagandists and of levellers. The latter, on the contrary, with greater reason perhaps, regard the English aristocracy as the corner-stone of the European social edifice, and as the greatest obstacle to their democratic schemes. This hatred with which England inspires the extreme parties might be expected to endear her to those more moderate; to the friends of well-ordered progress, of the gradual and regular development of humanity; to those, in short, who are in principle opposed equally to the violent upturning of society, and to its being kept in rigid incapacity of change. The fact is not so. The motives which might well induce sympathy with England are opposed by a host of prejudices, of memories, and of passions whose force is almost always irresistible. I do not wish to condemn all the causes of this hostility; I simply state the fact, because it explains the general excitement displayed regarding Ireland, when it has been thought that the agitation which has sprung up there endangered the existence of the British empire.

This sentiment is assuredly not the only cause of the sympathy felt on the continent for the Irish people; to assert this were a slander on humanity. That sympathy has its chief source in the generous instinct which leads individuals, as well as the masses of men, to feel interested in real suffering, and in affliction undeserved. Still, one may believe, without fear of injustice, that the hatred of the oppressors is not foreign to the sympathy of the European public with the oppressed.

In truth, we hear every day men the least favourable to liberty and toleration cry out loudly against English tyranny, and the sad condition of the Irish Catholics, while they have not a word of pity for their Polish co-religionists, victims of the religious persecutions of the Emperor of Russia. On the other hand, again and again, we meet with radicals who declaim with their usual energy against the wicked abuses of the political and religious aristocracy in Ireland, but who are silent about the other and more revolting iniquities of the aristocracy of skin in the country pre-eminently democratic.

It is of the very highest importance to explore the true causes of the movement which stirs men's minds in favour of Ireland, in order to guard against their possible influence on our appreciation of passing events in that country, as well as of their consequences and their probable results. Error in this respect would be fatal if men of extreme opinions, aiming at the same end, without distinction of parties, were to succeed in impressing on continental nations their opinions as to the dangers which threaten England. If the prophecies of the *Gazette de France* and of the *National* were to lead astray in this matter the majority of French politicians, the maintenance of peace, so desirable for all, but especially for those who, like myself, have more faith in ideas than in cannons for improving the lot of humanity, would become from day to day more difficult, and finally impossible. So soon as the masses shall be persuaded that the British power is weakened; that, undermined at its base, the colossus is no longer able to maintain, as in the past, a war of giants against a continental coalition,—all the efforts of states-men, all the resistance of peaceful interests will be powerless to arrest the flood of popular passions, which, taking the occasion as propitious for gratifying their antipathy to England and for revenging ancient wrongs, will hurry irresistibly the nations of Europe into a terrible struggle, as ruinous to their material interests as to their intellectual progress.

Notwithstanding what I have said regarding excessive prejudices against England, I cannot enter upon the subject which I purpose to treat, without frankly expressing my sympathy for that Irish people to whom long past generations have bequeathed a grievous heritage of misery and suffering. The wish not to be unjust to the powerful nation with which they are united by a bond which they wish to break, will not, I trust, make me insensible to their wrongs and indifferent to the cause of the evils, whose oppressive reality cannot be denied. If, from political considerations of a higher order, I were to think it imprudent to express the strong interest with which Ireland fills me, I would abandon the task which I have imposed upon myself, for, however grave those considerations might be, there are sentiments which even to them ought never to be sacrificed.

All the world knows the long and melancholy history of the miseries of Ireland. For eight centuries this country has endured every kind of oppression and of persecution. At first there were the evils of the barbarous conquest, the oppression of the Celtic by the Anglo-Norman race. After the conquest came the continual wars and revolts, which renewed at short intervals the disasters of the first invasion. Ireland of the middle age, always conquered, was never completely subdued. Those powerful Norman barons, whose domination had extended over the whole of England, and had banished the very shadow of Saxon nationality, could not succeed in establishing their empire on the same basis on the other side of St. George's Channel. The vast marshes of Ireland, its immense thickets stretching towards the west, in Connaught especially, for centuries offered a sure refuge to the indomitable Celts, and allowed them to maintain a savage independence at the cost of poverty and suffering of every kind.

From the conquest of Henry II. to the reign of Elizabeth, the history of Ireland is only a long succession of
rebellions, always defeated and always renewed. During
this period, the English were rather encamped than established in Ireland. Their real dominion never went beyond
the province of Leinster, the nearest to England. Beyond
its limits they exercised a sort of sovereignty usually
confined to a few ravaging excursions, prompted rather by
the spirit of vengeance than by the love of pillage. Those
four centuries were, for three-fourths of Ireland, only a
long war, which, in spite of numberless reverses, could not
effect the complete submission of the inhabitants. It is
perhaps in those fierce struggles that the energetic and
tenacious character of the Irish was formed. They owe
to the habits contracted in that period of incessant battles,
the marvellous persistence which has enabled them, when
material resistance became impossible, to preserve unchanged even to our time, thanks to an invincible moral
resistance, their national customs, faith, and physiognomy.

In spite of the admiration excited by the generous
efforts of the Irish to maintain their independence, we are
compelled to admit that it would have been well for them
had they been thoroughly subdued in the reign of Henry
II. Had the Norman barons once settled and consolidated
their sway over the Celtic population of Ireland, they
would no longer have regarded themselves as the chiefs of
an army encamped in a conquered country; they would in
time have become attached to their new country, and they
would have endowed it with beneficent institutions, such
as, from the middle ages onward, ensured the prosperity
and the glory of England. Four centuries would have
been more than enough to fuse the conquering and the

conquered races, so that, when their religious disputes broke out, these would not have been frightfully envenomed by the antipathies of race and nationality.

From the time of Elizabeth's reign, religious persecution took the place of the political persecution of the Irish people, or, to speak more truly, the one aggravated the other. Unalterably attached to the faith of their fathers, the people energetically resisted the repeated efforts for conversion made by the English government, which by turns resorted to violence and to corruption. They resisted openly under Elizabeth; conquered, they resisted secretly under James I. and Charles I.; and they suffered equally from the haughty domination of the last of the Tudors, and from the legal quibbles and the hypocritical cruelties of the first two Stuarts.

When the parliamentary revolution broke out, the Irish thought the time had come for revenge of the sufferings inflicted on them by the English during so many generations. They rose in mass to exterminate their oppressors, and committed frightful massacres. The horrible insurrection of 1641 was followed by wars still more horrible, by a reaction still more dreadful. The savage cruelty of the republican generals, the legal butcheries of Cromwell threw into the shade, if they did not justify, the crimes of the insurgents.*

Under the restoration, Ireland, defrauded of its legiti-

---

* See Clarendon's History of the Rebellion and Civil Wars, vol. 7, Oxford, 1749, Appendix: A Collection of *the Several* Massacres and Murders Committed *by* the Irish, since the 23rd of October, 1641.—pp. 209—222 (13 pages). A Collection of *Some* of the Massacres and Murders Committed *on* the Irish in Ireland, since the 23rd of October, 1641.—pp. 223—245 (22 pages),—*Translator*.

mate claims, was still in painful agitation, but without recourse to actual violence. It was attracted to the Stuarts by a secret instinct, though Charles II., more from weakness than from bad intent, abandoned his more faithful Catholic subjects to the suspicious tyranny of the English Protestants.

After the revolution of 1688, Ireland made one more effort to recover its independence. It fought for its king, for its faith, for its political existence. But fortune, as in former times, was unpropitious. Thoroughly defeated at the Boyne, exhausted and incapable of resistance, it fell again under the yoke of its oppressors.

The battle of the Boyne and the taking of Limerick were the last acts of the civil and religious wars which had for six centuries distracted and devastated Ireland. The English dominion was now firmly established over the whole island. Even Connaught, the last refuge of the insurgent Irish, was completely subdued. After the year 1690, war and bodily violence came to an end ; but to them succeeded legal tyranny, judicial persecutions, worse than the previous scourges, for they are equally oppressive and more degrading.

The reign of William III. and that of Queen Anne were occupied in building up, bit by bit, that monstrous legislation called the *penal law*, of which the avowed end was to maintain the Catholics in poverty and degradation, by crushing them at once in their faith, in their rights public and private, in their dearest affections. I will not here retrace that barbarous code. Since Ireland engaged the public attention, the journals have, from time to time, reproduced its most violent clauses, and they must be known to our readers.

The results of this inhuman code were lamentable. The cruelty was purely gratuitous, for, far from losing strength, Catholicism became all the stronger from the hatred with which the poor Irish regarded the religion of their oppressors. Every attempt at conversion failed. The English parliament, in the belief that it was promoting the established religion, merely, by its unjust laws, placed at the mercy of the rich Protestants, proprietors of the soil, the Catholic population which, in three-fourths of the country, were almost exclusively its cultivators. The penal laws which, at first, religious fanaticism had inspired, lost by degrees their primitive character, and, in the hands of those who applied them, became a means of social domination. During the greatest part of the eighteenth century, the Irish peasant was reduced to a state of slavery worse than that of the negro in the Antilles. Thanks to the anti-Catholic legislation, and to the manner in which it was applied, it was more difficult for him to obtain justice from a Protestant grand jury, than it is now for a slave in the French colonies to obtain it from the magistrates sent from the mother country to administer the laws. During this period, Ireland presents the saddest spectacle to be found in any civilised society,—complete and absolute oppression of the poor by the rich, of him who labours by him who possesses, organised by the law, and maintained by the ministers of justice.

When we reflect on the influence which such a state of things must have exercised on the relations of the different classes of society, we can better understand the difficulties of the present position of Ireland, and we easily discover the true origin of that profound antipathy and of that permanent hostility which even now, when all the penal laws have been repealed, render aliens to each other the Irish peasant and the proprietor of the soil, and which form the strongest obstacle in the path of those who strive sincerely for the material and moral improvement of the country.

When we reperuse the records of so many miseries and of so long oppression, we are drawn involuntarily to pass a severe judgment on the nation which was their author, or at least accomplice, and to demand from the present generation a reckoning for the barbarities of which their fathers were guilty. However moderate one may be, it is hard to resist the desire of seeing dawn for Ireland the day not only of justice but also of revenge. Nevertheless, if we subject this impulse of a generous indignation to the cool judgment of reason, we are forced to admit that the English of the time of William III. and of Queen Anne are not so culpable as they appear to us when we try them by the light of the nineteenth century. In persecuting the Catholics, in heaping vexation upon vexation so as to render their worship difficult and humiliating, the statesmen of that epoch were not conscious of the crime which they were perpetrating against humanity; they only followed the opinions of their time; they were rigorously faithful in applying the doctrines of intolerance which no one in Europe dared then openly to gainsay. Before condemning them too severely, let us remember that they were contemporary with the pious prelates who demanded and obtained the revocation of the edict of Nantes, and that they lived in a time when the promulgation of a black code, which now we cannot read without a shudder of horror, was reputed an eminently philanthropic act. Let us condemn, with all the energy of conviction that modern science can inspire, the cruel maxims, the false ideas which ruled the world a century ago ; but let us be indulgent to the men whose principal offence consisted in their inability to rise above the intelligence of their time, when the opinions generally received, far from checking their political passions, favoured and excited them.

When we compare the effect which the cruelties and the persecutions endured by Ireland produce upon us, children of the nineteenth century, with the effect which they produced on the most enlightened and refined of the last century, we cannot but rejoice at the immense progress that has occurred in the moral sense of nations.

On careful reflection, we shall be forced to own that this mere progress ought to render us indulgent towards our own times, and, while banishing regret for a past too little studied, to make us patient under the evils, often very serious, and always trying, of the period of transition through which modern societies are destined to pass.

During the first half of the eighteenth century, the spirit of toleration made considerable progress in Great Britain. The contemporaries of Locke and of Hume*

---

* In this reference to "the contemporaries of Locke and of Hume" there seems to be some confusion of dates. Locke, indeed, who was born in 1632, and who died in 1704, may well have exerted some influence on opinion "during the first half of the eighteenth century," for his First Letter on Toleration appeared in 1688. But Hume, who died in 1776, was not born till 1711; his Treatise on Human Nature appeared in 1738; the first part of his Essays in 1742; and his Political Discourses, Essays, and Inquiries concerning Morals in 1752. Of the earliest of these works he has himself recorded : "Never was literary attempt more unfortunate than my Treatise on Human Nature. It fell dead-born from the press, without reaching such distinction as even to excite a murmur among the zealots."—*Translator.*

could not cherish towards dissenters in religion the persecuting zeal which inflamed the disciples of Milton. The penal laws to which the Irish Catholics were subjected, came gradually to be regarded in their true light by most enlightened men in the country, and their abolition was demanded with growing energy by public opinion, that imponderable force which has so wonderful an action on the complicated springs of the British constitution.

Although there was an Irish parliament in Dublin, political reforms really depended on the will of England. In fact, the Irish legislature, in virtue of ancient statutes, of which the most important is known under the name of Poynings, the lieutenant of Henry VII., was so dependent on the government at London, that it was only an instrument in its hands. So long as the Stuart party preserved a spark of life, all relief was refused to the Irish Catholics, who were regarded as its most devoted partisans. When this party was utterly extinct, the government showed towards them a more favourable disposition. But it was not till the war of independence in America had shaken at home the power of Lord North's ministry, in 1778, that the partisans of religious toleration could make a partial breach in the monstrous edifice of penality which the hatred of Catholicism had built up in Ireland.

The influence of the American revolution was not confined to the reform of the penal laws; it made itself felt above all by the Protestant population of Ireland. Till then that population had patiently borne the political yoke of England, without whose aid it could not have forcibly maintained its religious supremacy and its civil domination over the Catholic population. It had consented to sacrifice its political rights in exchange for the needful means of retaining under the yoke of servitude the majority of their countrymen professing another creed. The movement begun in men's minds by this memorable struggle, aided by the progress of tolerant and liberal ideas, changed the disposition of the Irish Protestants, and led them to claim national independence.

The circumstances were eminently favourable. The British government, having all its regular forces employed in the colonies, was obliged, in order to preserve Ireland from the invasion with which it was threatened, to appeal to the wealthier classes in that country, and to organise among them militia-bands which took the name of united volunteers. These troops formed in the aggregate an imposing force, which preserved the country from foreign war, and which, at the same time, enabled the Irish to demand from the British parliament their political emancipation, in a way not to be resisted.

The triumph of the volunteers was accomplished in 1782. The ministry of Mr. Fox declared that the British parliament had never had the right to make laws for Ireland, or to invade the independence of the Irish parliament. This was to abdicate, officially at least, all idea of supremacy and of domination. It was the complete emancipation of Ireland, the abolition of the tutorial power which Britain had assumed.

The movement of 1782 was essentially Protestant ; the Catholics took no active part in it ; they applauded but did not effectively aid it. Nevertheless, the spirit which had animated the volunteers was too generous not to have an influence, at the moment of triumph at least, on the condition of the Catholics. One of the first acts of the

Irish parliament, after achieving its independence, was to repeal a part of the penal laws which the reform of 1778 had left in force.

However glorious for Ireland may have been the peaceful revolution effected in 1782, we must not exaggerate its significance; it was far from establishing in fact the independence of the Irish nation. The parliament at Dublin was, it is true, declared sovereign and all powerful, as fully as the British parliament; but, its internal composition not having been changed, it had really only a shadow of independence. In fact the Irish Chamber of Commons was mainly composed of the representatives of rotten boroughs, and of municipal corporations, which admitted only a very small number of persons, all devoted to the Protestant cause. Of three hundred members, the counties elected only twenty-four; the cities containing above six thousand souls, at most fifty; the rest were nominated by the great proprietors of boroughs, most of whom resided in England, where they were under the absolute control of the government.

It may be affirmed, without exaggeration, that the Irish parliament, even after 1782, was of legislative bodies the most corruptible and the most corrupt. Certainly there were glorious exceptions, names pure from all taint;* long lives that no suspicion could assail; but those rare exceptions render still more striking the servility and corruptness of the majority of that political body which they vainly adorned.

The united volunteers, after having obtained the national independence, demanded a parliamentary reform; but, it

---

* Such were those of Grattan and Lord Charlemont.

must be owned, on this point they displayed much less ardour and unanimity. Many of their body feared to enter on the career of internal reforms, in the name of the great principles of equity and justice, for they felt that it must inevitably lead to the emancipation of the Catholics, and in this they took no interest. Nevertheless, as ideas of toleration made new progress from day to day, it is probable that the sincere Irish reformers would finally have triumphed over religious prejudices and antipathies, if the war of the French revolution had not arisen to disturb the regular development of liberal principles in England. The statesmen, indeed, of that country felt strongly the necessity of making in the English constitution the changes which the progress of the times demanded. Mr. Pitt, it is well known, though the minister of a king not friendly to innovations, declared, so early as 1785, for a large and effective parliamentary reform. Before the events in France had turned aside his projects of reform, this he would probably have accomplished, but for the unfortunate illness of George III. and the avowed hostility of the Prince of Wales.

If Pitt had effected his plan of parliamentary reform, he would without doubt have extended it to Ireland; and this measure would have been the greatest of benefits to that country, for it would have been impossible to touch the political edifice which the Protestants had raised on a narrow, false, and factitious basis, without recognising and conceding the rights of the Catholics.

Had parliamentary reform and Catholic emancipation been accomplished in Ireland before 1792, before revolutionary passions had agitated that country and revived the ancient hatred of its sects and races, it would have been saved from a long series of sufferings and calamities of which the end, alas! has not yet come. Providence did not permit those healing measures to be then applied; Ireland was destined to become, after a long career of misery, an inexhaustible source of anxieties and troubles to its oppressors, in order perhaps, to give to the world a great lesson, and to teach the most powerful nations that their crimes and their errors recoil sooner or later on those who commit them.

The French revolution surprised the Irish reformers at the outset of their efforts, and arrested their course. In 1792 they achieved, indeed, the repeal of the remaining penal enactments which still weighed upon the Catholics, and obtained the right of voting at elections; an immense concession, which would necessarily have brought about their complete emancipation, if the country had continued to advance in the way of regular and peaceful regeneration, which the events consequent on the American revolution appeared to have opened up.

The outbreaks of the democratic spirit in France, the horrible excesses of 1793, produced a complete reaction in the rich and enlightened classes of England and of Ireland. The volunteers were disbanded without opposition, without even a protest by their chiefs against this measure. Most of the reformers of 1782 became determined conservatives, so soon as social order seemed threatened by the terrible propagandism of anarchy which the Convention sought to organise. The events in France, however, the effect of which had been to detach the higher classes from the reforming party, drove the rest of that party headlong into revolutionary ways. The remnants of the volunteers formed a secret association under the name of "United Irishmen," who endeavoured to unite all the lower classes, without distinction of race or creed, for subversive ends. The ultra democratic and republican tendencies of this association, its avowed intention to follow the example of France, kept aloof from it all men who, by their intelligence, their rank, or their riches, held a place in the least distinguished in society.

The United Irishmen, blinded by their passions, exaggerating their strength and number, and above all reckoning on efficient aid from France, which the misdoings of the rulers of that country and the opposition of the elements did not permit them to obtain, attempted an insurrectionary movement in 1798. The issue was not for an instant doubtful. Without leaders, without orders, without prepared plans, the insurgents could only commit frightful outrages, and inflict terrible vengeance on those whom they viewed as their greatest enemies—the Protestants and the English. Nowhere did they succeed in organising a serious resistance ; as soon as the English army took the field, they dispersed almost without a blow.

The repression enforced by the government was cruel ; it resembled rather ferocious reprisals than justice severely but reluctantly applied to misguided subjects. Nevertheless it attained its end : the revolutionary spirit was crushed, the reforming party was destroyed, only feeble but brilliant fragments remained.

The insurrection of 1798 supplied to the great minister who then guided the destinies of Great Britain—Mr. Pitt—the pretext and the means for carrying into effect a measure which he must long have meditated. In that war to the death which he carried on with the colossal

C

power of France, he could not fail to be struck more than once with the dangers caused to England by the legislative independence of Ireland, and he must have eagerly desired to be able to unite the two parliaments of London and of Dublin. Public opinion in England declared loudly in favour of this union, and the parliament supplied to the ministry all the means needful for its accomplishment.

There was a great obstacle to be overcome : the consent of the Irish parliament must be obtained ; it must be induced itself to pronounce its sentence of death. Mr. Pitt thought he could carry this measure with a high hand ; but at the first attempt he failed. The first project of legislative union, presented in 1799, was rejected by the Irish House of Commons. The ministry had then recourse to a means which it had found always successful in the parliament of Dublin : it practised corruption on an immense scale. It bought a large number of rotten boroughs ; it lavished places, honours, pensions, and, at the end of a year, it procured a majority of one hundred and sixty-eight votes against seventy-three, for the union of the Irish parliament with that of Great Britain.

Let us pause for a few moments to examine this celebrated act, which has at all times called forth in Ireland complaints so bitter, and recriminations so violent, and which is, at this day, the pretext, if not the cause, of the agitation which shakes this country to its deepest roots.

We must, at the outset, distinguish the merits of this measure in itself from the means employed for its accomplishment. There can be but one voice in condemning to infamy those who made traffic of the independence of their country, who bartered their rights and their political influence against gold and places, who sold their vote and sanctioned an act which their conscience disapproved. But must we equally condemn the government which purchased those corrupt men? I would not hesitate to do this if, by a fatal error, public opinion in ages past, and even in our own, had not in some measure sanctioned on the part of government a morality different from that which private persons recognise ; if it had not, in all times, treated with excessive indulgence the immoral acts which have brought about great political results. If we would brand with disgrace the character of Pitt for having practised parliamentary corruption on a great scale, we must treat with equal severity the greatest monarchs of past times, Louis XIV., Joseph II., the great Frederick, who, to reach their ends, offended far more grievously against the inflexible principles of morality and of humanity than did the illustrious statesman who established the United Kingdom of Great Britain and Ireland.

But, putting aside the appreciation of the conduct and the merits of those who took part in the act of union, let us examine this measure in itself, and let us see if, in fact, it has been unjust and iniquitous towards Ireland, and if it deserves all the hatred which it excites even at this day, all the vituperation which O'Connell and the orators of the popular party lavish upon it without ceasing.

For myself, I declare frankly that I do not think so. In accomplishing the legislative union of the British islands Pitt was not moved by a narrow desire of domination; he did not act in the exclusive interest of one political party or of one religious sect. It was not in order to enslave Ireland, to impose upon it his despotic will, that he sought to unite all the parliamentary powers under one roof at Westminster. If such had been his object, he would surely not have needed to incur such odium to effect the union of the two countries; he knew very well that the Irish parliament, composed as it was, was but an instrument in his skilful and firm hands. The insurrection of 1798 had taught the Protestants, who alone constituted the legal country, that their existence depended wholly on the support of England, and that without the continual aid of English bayonets, they would have been the victims of the spirit of hatred and of vengeance which animated the immense majority of the Catholic population. The consciousness of its weakness, therefore, made the party which exclusively composed the Irish parliament, absolutely dependent on the cabihet at London. In order to exercise over it a complete domination, Pitt would not have needed to resort to the ancient methods of corruption; intimidation would have sufficed. By forcing it to commit suicide, he exacted from the parliament the only act which could encounter a serious resistance; and as regards himself, he lost rather than gained in parliamentary influence.

The aim of Pitt was noble and great. By uniting under the same government the two islands which St. George's Channel severs, he hoped to strengthen, to consolidate the edifice of British power, then exposed to terrible attacks. He realised the thought of one of those men who have possessed in the highest degree the instinct of government—Cromwell—who nearly two centuries before, desired to fuse the parliament of Ireland with that of Britain. But, if the dominant thought was to strengthen the government by simplifying the machinery of legislation, he thought also, I dare affirm, of performing an act useful to Ireland, by withdrawing it from the dominion of a blind and persecuting church. He wished to give to the

Catholics, by means of the parliament of the united kingdom, complete political emancipation, which they would never have obtained from the Irish parliament. If he did not realise these generous plans, it was because he found in the will of George III. an obstacle which he had not the courage to surmount, at a time when the support of the crown was to him indispensable in order to save the nationality of his country, threatened by the power of France.

A very false estimate of this illustrious statesman commonly prevails. It is a grave error to represent him as the patron of all abuses, of all oppressions, like a Lord Eldon, or a Prince of Polignac. Far from it; Pitt had all the enlightenment of his time ; the son of Chatham was not the friend of despotism, or the champion of religious intolerance. With an intellect powerful and wide, he loved power as a means, not as an end. He began his political life by opposing the retrograde administration of Lord North ; and, as soon as he was himself a minister, one of his first acts was to proclaim the necessity of a reform in parliament. Pitt, assuredly, had not one of those ardent souls which are passionately devoted to the great interests of humanity, which, when they see these in question, regard neither the obstacles in their way, nor the troubles which their zeal may bring upon them. He was not one of those men who wish to reconstruct society from bottom to top, by means of general notions and humanitarian theories. A genius profound and cold, void of prejudices, he was animated solely by the love of his country, and by the love of glory. At the outset of his career, he saw the defects in the body politic, and he set himself to correct them. If he had continued to wield power in a period of peace and of tranquility, he would have been a reformer after the fashion of Mr. Peel and Mr. Canning, combining the boldness and the large views of the one with the wisdom and ability of the other.

But as soon as he saw gathering in the horizon the storm of the French revolution, he foresaw, with the perspicacity of superior intelligence, the outbreak of demagogic principles and the dangers which they would bring on England. He stopped short at once in his projects of reform, in order to provide for the crisis which was preparing. He knew that in presence of the movement of revolutionary ideas which threatened to invade England, it would have been imprudent to touch the sacred ark of the constitution, and, by trying to repair the mouldering parts of the social edifice which time had consecrated, to weaken the respect with which it inspired the nation. From the day when the revolution, overflowing the country in which it had arisen, menaced Europe, Pitt had only one object in view, to resist France, and to prevent ultra-democratic ideas from invading England. To this supreme interest he devoted all his means ; to this he sacrificed every other political consideration.

Pitt's conduct, from the English point of view, cannot be too highly praised. By opposing France, by repressing at home the violence of demagogues, he saved the social order of England, and kept civilisation in the ways of regular progress and of continuous development, which up to that time it had pursued ;—for there does not now exist a single individual, among persons of the least good sense, be he radical or declared partisan of repeal, who could dare to deny the fearful consequences which a democratic revolution, if accomplished at the end of last century, would have brought upon Great Britain.

By abandoning his thoughts of reform, by becoming conservative in the largest sense of the word, Pitt did not constitute himself the defender of injustice and oppression. I think I find a proof of this assertion in the very act of union which has been the object of so many reproaches and recriminations. Let us examine its chief provisions, and see if the English ministry abused the unlimited power which the terror caused by the insurrection of 1798, and the means of corruption which it had employed, placed in its hands,—to give to England the lion's share in the legislative union by it effected, and to treat Ireland rather as a conquered country than as a portion of the same empire.

These chief provisions may be summed up in the eight following articles:

1. The two kingdoms of England and Ireland are declared to form one sole kingdom, under the title of Great Britain and Ireland.

2. The succession to the throne of the United Kingdom shall continue to be regulated by the laws now in force.

3. The United Kingdom shall be represented by one parliament only, which shall take the name of the parliament of Great Britain and Ireland.

4. Twenty-eight Irish temporal peers, elected for life by the whole body of peers, as well as four bishops succeeding each other in turn, shall be admitted to the House of Lords of the United Kingdom; and Ireland shall send one hundred members to the House of Commons; that is to say,—sixty-four members elected by the thirty-two counties, one by the University of Dublin, four by the cities of Dublin and Cork, and thirty-one by thirty-one of the most important towns or boroughs.

5. The churches of England and Ireland shall be united and shall form only one church, subject to the same laws, the same doctrines, to the same discipline as the national Church of England.

6. The subjects of the two nations shall be placed on the same footing in all that relates to industry, to commerce and navigation.

7. England and Ireland shall contribute to the general expenses of the state in the proportion of fifteen to two; this distribution shall last twenty years, and after that time, the expenses shall be redistributed by parliament.

8. The laws now in force and the courts of justice shall continue to exist as hitherto, except that appeals from the Irish Courts of Chancery shall be carried to the House of Lords of the United Kingdom.

It appears at once that, as regards the civil and economic relations of the two kingdoms, the act of union is irreproachable. England and Ireland are placed by it on a footing of the most absolute equality. If there were sacrifices or concessions on either side, it is by England that they were made, since it consented to open its colonies to Ireland, and to share the benefits of a monopoly of which it alone had the privilege.

As regards religion, the union is less favourable to the majority of the Irish nation; I do not hesitate to say that it made the condition worse. But let it not be forgotten that England treated in Ireland with "the legal country," composed exclusively of Protestants, who would never have consented to dispossess themselves of the power which they exercised, if their religious privileges had not been guaranteed to them in their integrity.

The points which I have now examined are only

subsidiary; the essential provisions of the Act of Union are those which regulate the proportion of political power reserved to each of the two countries, and the manner in which the public burdens are divided between them.

Of the six hundred and fifty-eight members of which the House of Commons was composed after the union, Ireland was to have a hundred, and Great Britain five hundred and fifty-eight. In the House of Lords, Ireland obtained thirty-two representatives. Finally, its share of the public burdens was fixed at two-seventeenths of the total outlay. Was this an unfair division—an abuse of power; were these conditions humiliating, and such as might be imposed by an insolent victor on a vanquished people? A few moments' reflection will suffice to convince us of the reverse.

I confess that the number of representatives granted to the Irish peers seems at first disproportionate, especially if we look to the number of persons that now constitute the House of Lords. But we must remember that in 1800 that number was much smaller than it is at present; so that the inequality was far less than that which strikes us when we think of thirty-two Irish peers now sitting among four hundred British peers. In spite of this seeming injustice, I cannot blame this provision of the Act of Union. In fact, the Irish peerage was much less illustrious and eminent than the British peerage. With a few exceptions, its ranks had been filled almost exclusively by the most servile and devoted instruments of British domination. Never had it done a popular act. Its suppression was a real service to the country. The introduction into the House of Lords of a certain number of Irish Peers was far from being a benefit to Ireland.

Since 1800, and even to our day, they have always been the most violent, the most backward of the Tory party, the most opposed to every sort of concession or reform.

The successive ministers from Pitt to the present time have called to the House of Lords very many Irish peers; there are now more than fifty besides the thirty-two representatives of the Irish peerage. I cannot think that the true friends of Ireland have had reason to rejoice in this seeming favour bestowed upon that country.

As to the composition of the House of Commons, according to the terms of the union, Ireland having a hundred deputies, while England and Scotland retained five hundred and fifty-eight, its political influence was to that of Britain in the ratio of 1 to 5·58. This is too small if we compare the populations of the two countries at that epoch. In 1800, England and Scotland reckoned eleven millions of inhabitants. We do not know exactly the number of the Irish people at that time, but we can scarcely estimate it at less than four millions. The populations of the two countries were then one to the other as 4 is to 11, or rather as 1 to 2·75, while their ratio of political influence was as 1 to 5·58. If, then, we reason according to the mathematical ideas which the French revolution made current, there is here a flagrant injustice to Ireland.

There are, however, two things to be considered which, in great measure at least, exonerate the authors of the Act of Union from the charge of unfairness to Ireland in this respect.

In the first place, as the census had not, in 1800, been yet taken in Ireland, the population of that country was supposed to be much less numerous than it really was.

An official document published in 1785 stated the number
of inhabitants at 2,845,000. It was, then, natural that
statesmen, charged with the partition of political influence
between the two countries, should take this number as the
basis of their calculations. The populations of the two
countries were thus stated to be in the ratio of 1 to 3·86,
so that the apparent injustice done to Ireland was reduced
by one third.

But, in the second place, it must be borne seriously in
mind that in Britain never has the number of the
population been considered as the only element to be
taken into account in the distribution of political rights.
In the middle ages, the chief office of the House of
Commons being to vote subsidies, it was composed exclusively of representatives of the commons who were able
to pay taxes. During several centuries, it was rather the
guardian of the national purse, than an integral portion
of the supreme power. Time and revolutions have, it is
true, strangely modified this idea; nevertheless it has
left its traces in the British constitution, and even at this
day it exerts a certain influence in that country.

If, accordingly, the public wealth, or, what comes to
the same thing, if the distribution of the public burdens
had been taken as the basis of the distribution of legislative power, Ireland would not have had reason to complain,
since it contributed to the finances of the kingdom less
than an eighth of the taxation, while it obtained the sixth
part of the representation of the United Kingdom.

By comparing all the ciphers which I have cited, we
find that the number of deputies granted to Ireland by the
Act of Union is a sort of mean proportion between what
would have accrued had the number of the population,

and what would have accrued had the amount of taxation, been taken as the basis of the distribution of legislative power.

Notwithstanding all that I have said, I do not maintain the absolute justice, the perfect equity of this important part of the Act of Union; but I do not hesitate to affirm that it is in all respects conformable to the practical notions of political equity and justice at that time generally prevalent in England. I have not the least doubt that if strictly impartial arbiters, chosen, however, among politicians imbued with English doctrines, had been instructed to determine the proportion which Britain and Ireland respectively should have in the united parliament, they would not have treated Ireland more liberally than did Pitt.

After 1800, Ireland was governed like the rest of the British empire by the three estates sitting at Westminster. Did the great majority of the country, the Catholics especially, lose much by this political change, and have they had serious reasons to regret their national parliament? This cannot be maintained. The parliament of Dublin, as I have already said, was composed exclusively in the Protestant interest. Notwithstanding the right granted to the Catholics, in 1792, of voting at elections, they could never have exerted any influence on the House of Commons, for, with the exception of the counties which elected but a small part of the members composing the house (sixty-four out of three hundred), their right was quite illusory. In the twenty-six towns of any importance that returned deputies, the right of election was reserved to the municipal corporations, that is to say to the utmost violence and intolerance ever exhibited by the spirit of prejudiced fanaticism.   As to the small boroughs, for which one hundred and twenty-four deputies had been reserved, they were absolutely dependent on a few oligarchs who, disposing of the majority of the house, usually united so as to sell their votes to the British government, with the greatest advantage to themselves.

It is not such an assembly as that that the great national Irish party wishes to resuscitate.   I much doubt that they would consent to its revival, even if the repeal of the Act of Union were to be obtained on this condition. If they did consent, it would be with the secret hope of soon crushing, under the weight of the popular indignation, an assembly so anti-national.   But if, while granting to Ireland the restoration of its ancient parliament, the British government placed at the disposal of that body a numerous army to repress the attempts of extra-legal reform by the Catholic party, we may well believe that in Ireland there would be but one voice to demand the maintenance of the existing order of things, which, though far from being satisfactory, is still greatly preferable to that to which it succeeded.   The ancient edifice of the Irish constitution, let it never be forgotten, was a monstrous assemblage of injustice and iniquities; since it was not possible to reform it, its destruction was a deed well done. Therefore it is that, all things considered, I must regard the Act of Union, in spite of all its defects, as an event at which humanity must rejoice.

In opposition to this assertion, which will appear strange to all those who are content to study history in the daily newspapers, will be cited the example of 1782, and it will be contended that if the union had not taken place, the Catholics would have obtained religious emancipation and parliamentary reform by the same means which the volunteers had successfully employed to wrest from Britain the recognition of national independence. But this would be a serious error. In 1782, Ireland was unanimous; she had on her side justice, strength, and a certain measure of legality. Britain, enfeebled by a disastrous war, had herself put arms into her hands, and had helped her to organise an imposing military force. How, in those circumstances, could the British government have refused demands which, besides, were approved by the public opinion of the whole country? But, after the French revolution had broken out, the Protestant party in a body declared against every kind of reform. Holding absolute mastery of parliament, they would long have refused the slightest concessions in favour of the Catholics.

Mr. Pitt, it must in justice be said, regarded the Act of Union as the only means of consolidating religious peace in Ireland, and of establishing there an equitable political system. He had promised to the Catholics to present to the parliament of the united kingdoms, so soon as it should be constituted, an act to restore. to them the exercise of all their rights. In his eyes their emancipation was a necessary consequence of the fusion of the two countries. Unhappily his projects of conciliation and of tolerance met an almost insuperable obstacle in the obstinacy and narrow prejudices of the old king, George III. At first he showed himself faithful to the true principles of parliamentary government, and he quitted office rather than renounce the execution of his promises towards the Catholics. But he was faithful to them only by half. When restored to the ministry by his old lieutenants, he did not use the immense parliamentary influence at his disposal to secure the triumph of the principles of religious toleration which he had proclaimed. Exclusively pre-occupied with the external dangers which threatened England, he aimed at regaining power, less in the interest of her internal policy than in order to sustain with greater energy and vigour the terrible struggle which he had begun with France. At this decisive moment he wished not to weaken his means of action by alienating the confidence of his aged sovereign. He sacrificed the Catholics to the success of his political war.

Britain committed an enormous fault in not granting to the Catholics emancipation as a consequence of the Act of Union. It would by this means have secured their attachment, or, at least, would have rendered less unpopular with the great mass of the nation a measure which could not fail to wound the national pride of Ireland. Emancipation would not have healed all the wounds of Ireland ; but it would have prevented their being more and more envenomed. The poor and suffering classes, instead of attributing all their evils to the British parliament, would have been accustomed to regard it as a just and protecting power; and they would have patiently waited to receive from it what to them was much more necessary than political rights : great ecclesiastical and social reforms.

So long as the war with Napoleon lasted, the parliament had neither time nor inclination to take up questions of reform, whether in Britain or in Ireland. The Whigs, during their short period of power, did nothing for the latter country. After the peace, the prodigious success obtained by the government had given to the Tory party, who claimed, not without some reason, the monopoly of the national glory, so great strength that all reform

seemed to be indefinitely postponed. The emancipation
of the Catholics, which in 1800 had been on the point of
accomplishment, was regarded in 1817 as a thing impossible.

Nevertheless, the fruitful germs of progress and of
liberty inherent in the British constitution, though kept
down for a time by the intoxication of victory, soon began
to spring up anew. The spirit of reform, stifled by the
cares of war and then by the joys of triumph, awoke
with fresh strength, and on all sides broke out complaints,
more and more energetic, against the glaring political
inequalities sanctioned by the constitution. The ablest
and the most enlightened of the Tories felt the gravity of
this movement, and thought that the time had come to
grant some of the demands of the popular party. Canning
and his friends, impressed by this conviction, introduced
into their party and into the ministry the principle of
reform, and ardently espoused the cause of religious
toleration.

During all this time the Irish Catholics, breathing freely
in a state of civil liberty, had largely increased in numbers,
in wealth, and in intelligence. Their leaders had learned
that the time for revolts and for violent revolutions had
passed—that their only reasonable hope lay in the skilful
and persevering use of the legal means which the British
constitution, to its glory be it said, places within reach of
the suffering classes, to obtain redress of their grievances.
For this end a committee was organised in Dublin so early
as in 1810, to support by the press, or in all other legal
ways, the claims of the Catholics. This committee, at
first guided during several years by John Keogh, extended
its ramifications over the whole of Ireland. It grew up in

darkness and in silence, and, before, so to speak, the British government was aware of its existence, it had organised throughout the country an immense association embracing almost the entire Catholic population.

This celebrated association, known under the name of the Catholic Association, perfectly disciplined by its skilful chief, the illustrious O'Connell, suddenly, in 1825, displayed itself in a startling manner. Its imposing attitude, the astonishing power which it wielded over the Irish masses, produced in Britain an immense effect. It succeeded in organising and in maintaining an agitation so threatening, without, however, transgressing the bounds of legality, that after some years the government was reduced to the alternative of crushing it by force, or of disarming it by concessions. The leaders of the Tory party, then in power, after long hesitation, adopted the latter course. The Duke of Wellington and Mr. Peel, who, a few years before, had separated from Canning, rather than follow him in the new path which he wished to take in home politics, resolved to grant to the Irish Catholics all their demands. This decision was wise and prudent, rather than generous. In fact, if they yielded, it was because they perceived that the British nation would not long have supported them, if, in order to maintain Protestant supremacy in Ireland, they had been obliged to resort to violent means, such as were employed against the reformers of the sixteenth and eighteenth centuries.

The Act of 1829, drawn up by Mr. Peel, who, more than any other statesman, is instinctively aware of the necessities of the moment, was complete. The political incapacity which had for centuries oppressed the Catholics,

D

was entirely abolished. The only restrictions were that they were excluded from the offices of the Regent of the kingdom, the Lord Lieutenant of Ireland, the Chancellors of England and of Ireland, and the President of the General Assembly of the Church of Scotland—exclusions based on solid reasons, and neither unjust nor insulting to the Catholics of Great Britain.

Nevertheless, the Act of Emancipation, wrested from the fear, rather than due to the good will, of parliament, did not content Ireland. Her inveterate sores required deeper remedies than a simple political reform, which the Irish patriots with reason regarded rather as a means for obtaining the redress of their country's wrongs, than as in itself the end of their efforts. The agitation, further stimulated by the events of July, 1830, began anew with greater intensity and violence than before.

O'Connell, then all powerful with his party, engaged in a memorable struggle with the government of Lord Grey, and the consequences seemed likely to be serious. But scarcely had the ministry brought forward the famous bill for parliamentary reform, when O'Connell desisted from all attack, from all hostile movement. Perceiving with instinctive and admirable sagacity the interest which the Catholics had in the success of that measure, he passed, with surprising dexterity, from an almost factious opposition, to boundless devotion to the Whig party.

So long as the fate of the bill was doubtful, so long as reform was not decided, Lord Grey had no more sure and faithful allies than the Irish Catholic members. To them must be attributed a considerable part of the victory which that minister, supported by public opinion, gained over the House of Lords.

The Reform Bill did something for Ireland, and especially for the Catholics. To Ireland five new representatives were granted; one for the University of Dublin, and four for towns whose importance had increased. But, what was of more consequence, the electoral franchise was extended. It had hitherto been concentrated in the boroughs and placed in the hands of municipal corporations, wholly composed of Protestants and of fanatical Protestants. It was now extended to every inhabitant paying ten pounds in rent. This change secured to the Catholics the majority in most of the electoral bodies.

Parliamentary reform alone could not, any more than emancipation, dry up the springs of popular agitation in Ireland. Lord Grey erred in regarding it as the proper boundary of the legislation of the reforming party. This opinion, true in a certain measure relatively to England, was, in relation to Ireland, wholly false. To the Irish Catholics especially, it could be only a further means for obtaining the changes in the religious and social order which the state of their country imperiously demanded. From the year 1832, the agitation was revived in a form more than ever threatening. It was directed in particular against tithes, an impost which was odious to the Catholics from the humiliations which it inflicted, as from the pecuniary sacrifices which it involved. This time, O'Connell was not strong enough to keep the popular movement within legal bounds. The peasants, exasperated by misery and by the disappointment of their hopes of relief from tithes, waged a terrible war upon the clergy. The resistance to the collections of this impost was so well organised, and so vigorously maintained, that it became impossible for

the tithe agents to obtain payment, even with the aid of
the police and of regular troops. In vain the government
of Lord Grey endeavoured to quell this general resistance
by vigorous means. The powers with which it was armed
by the Coercion Bill of 1833, were not effective in obtaining for the clergy payment of their dues; and when, to
relieve the extreme distress into which that body had
fallen, the government took the tithes upon itself, its
efforts were not more successful.

The ministry was not unanimous as to the course to be
pursued with the Catholics. A certain number of members of the cabinet were disposed to concession; they
succeeded in laying before parliament, at the same time
as the Coercion Bill, a measure for initiating the reform of
the Anglican Church established in Ireland. In virtue of
this law, which, after long contests, was passed by both
houses, the Catholics were freed from the ecclesiastical
contribution named *Vestry Cess*, which the Protestants
had the right to levy from all the inhabitants of their
parish for the maintenance of their churches. The funds
arising from this impost were supplemented by a reserve
on the revenue of all ecclesiastical benefices, and by the
produce of ten bishoprics, and of some other ecclesiastical
charges, of which the suppression was decreed after the
death of the surviving holders.

This bill was a great boon to Catholic Ireland, less by
the reforms that it sanctioned, than by the precedent
which it established. The government, having touched
the sacred ark of the church, was on the way to be compelled by the force of things to reduce its revenues in
proportion to the real requirements of the small minority
that professes in Ireland the religion of the state.

In fact, the majority in the ministry were not slow in an endeavour to draw from the principle established by the bill of 1833 the logical consequences that flowed naturally from it. They pronounced themselves in favour of Mr. Ward's motion, which sought to make parliament declare that the state had the right to appropriate for secular uses the surplus revenues of the church. Four ministers, more Protestants than reformers, Lord Stanley, Sir James Graham, the Duke of Richmond, and Lord Goderich, refusing to subscribe to this declaration, quitted the cabinet. Soon afterwards, Lord Grey, who followed reluctantly the policy of his colleagues towards Ireland, imitated their example and abandoned office.

The retirement of the intractable Whig partisans of the established church, led to the ministry of Lord Melbourne, which, with the exception of the very short interval of the vain attempt of the Peel ministry, governed England during six years. The formation of the Melbourne ministry was a great event for Ireland. In fact, it was formed avowedly to satisfy her just demands. For the first time the fall of a ministry had been caused by their refusal to grant the wishes of the Irish people, and a new cabinet had proclaimed aloud the intention to treat Catholics and Protestants on a footing of equality. For the first time, in the course of centuries, Catholics were called to assume the first dignities of the magistracy. The nomination of Mr. O'Loughlen to the Mastership of the Rolls—the second place in the Courts of Equity—and that of Mr. Sheil as member of the Privy Council, signalised the beginning of a new era for Ireland, from the date of which the Liberal party have wholly ceased to take religious differences into account.

Lord Melbourne confided the administration of Ireland to men of a firm and conciliatory disposition, who succeeded in gaining the esteem and the confidence of the Catholics. The two Lord Lieutenants during his ministry, Lord Mulgrave and Lord Fortescue, exercised power in the true interests of the country; through their justice and impartiality Ireland enjoyed an amount of tranquillity beyond all previous conception.

If Ireland owes much to those Lord Lieutenants, she owes still more to the true representative of the ministry, to the Secretary of State—Lord Morpeth—who, during six years, employed all the power with which he was invested to obliterate the traces of religious discords, and to cicatrise the wounds of that unhappy country. We may indulge the hope that the career of this statesman—the hope of the Whig party—will not close without his being permitted to complete, as minister or as Lord Lieutenant, the work of pacification and of regeneration which he has so worthily begun under the ministry of Lord Melbourne.

The legislative attempts of the ministry to improve the condition of the Catholics were not so successful as their efforts in administration. It was only by abandoning the application of the famous principle of the appropriation of the surplus revenues of the church that they could carry through both houses a measure for transmuting tithes into a perpetual rent charge, and they were obliged to return five times to the attack ere they could effect the reform of the Irish municipal corporations, and not without submitting to several amendments which impaired its efficacy.

In spite of the concessions which the ministry were forced to make, the two laws just mentioned were not less the source of great benefits to Ireland.

The law for the conversion of tithes reduced their amount to three-fourths of what they were when they were paid in kind. Besides, it levied this impost directly from the landowners; and thus put an end to the hateful relations between the ecclesiastical tithe-collectors and the wretched Catholic tenants. It is probable that the tithe now, as heretofore, falls in the last resort on the tenant; but as he does not pay it directly, and as it is confounded with the rent paid to the proprietor, the impost appears to him much less humiliating and vexatious. Since the promulgation of the new law for the conversion of tithes, peace, accordingly, has been no more disturbed in the agricultural districts, and the clergy of the established church have collected their revenues without obstacle or difficulty.

The reform of the municipal corporations, though less complete than that before made in England and in Scotland, has, nevertheless, been an immense triumph to the Catholics. These corporations were truly citadels in which found refuge the most passionate and fanatical spirit of intolerance and persecution exhibited in late times. By destroying their privileges, by granting the right of vote to all the electors with a certain guarantee of income, the law gave to the Catholics a preponderating influence in almost all the towns. It is to this law that the Catholics owed the satisfaction of seeing their illustrious leader, whom they justly name their Liberator—O'Connell— occupy the first municipal dignity of the kingdom, and, as Mayor of Dublin, take precedence of all the public functionaries, even the Lord Chancellor himself, in the train of the Lord Lieutenant.

During the whole period of the Melbourne ministry

the peace of Ireland was not broken. The conduct of
O'Connell and the other leaders of the Catholic party on
this occasion is above all praise. Renouncing the seductive
triumphs of popular agitation, they made as great efforts
to maintain the tranquillity which they had achieved as
they had made to originate the movement which caused
the retirement of Lord Grey.

Shortly after Queen Victoria ascended the throne in
the month of October, 1837, O'Connell induced the
Catholic Association to pass the following resolution,
which so well expresses the disposition of the Catholic
party at that time, that I think I must quote it in full :—

" The National Association, profoundly grateful for the
firm, energetic, humane, and perfectly impartial administration of Lord Mulgrave ;* fully confiding in the sincere
purpose of Her Majesty to render justice to Ireland, by
placing it on the same footing as England and Scotland ;
and, above all and before all, inspired with gratitude, as
respectful as lively, to Her Most Gracious Majesty, on
account of the national and enlightened policy which has
marked the beginning of her auspicious reign,—declares
its wish to give a striking testimony of its confidence in
the administration by dissolving itself, and by leaving
the realisation of its projects to the Irish and popular
members of parliament who support the government of
the Queen."

This resolution—so wise and so loyal, proposed by
O'Connell—contrasts strangely with the sentiments of
passionate hostility to which he had given frank utterance
some years before against England and against the Whigs

---

* Afterwards Lord Normanby.

themselves. We do not in this language recognise the man who, when he contended against the administration of Lord Grey, went so far in his anger as to advise his fellow-citizens, in order to diminish the resources of the government, to abstain from consuming any article subject to either excise or customs duty. And yet, under those seeming inconsistencies, we find a perfect harmony in O'Connell's plans. By a thousand means, which he could multiply without ceasing, and vary without end, according to the exigencies of the moment, he still advances to the same object—the political elevation of his fellow-religionists and fellow-countrymen. In consideration of the constancy of his moving principle, history will pardon his continual variations, his so various judgments of the same measures and the same men.

I have been careful to note those changes in the conduct of O'Connell and the party which follows him with a blind confidence, not only that I may throw light upon past events, but still more that I may make the present state of Ireland more intelligible, and disabuse the minds of those who, taking literally the energetic protests, the rash promises of which O'Connell during the past year has been so lavish, regard that country as irrevocably pledged to a deadly strife with Britain.

The calm and orderly conduct of the Irish since the formation of the Melbourne ministry, bears high testimony to the progress which the people have made in real civilisation. It sufficed that a government should show itself well disposed towards them, that it should display the intention to respect their beliefs, and not to shock their national sentiments; immediately this people, so turbulent, so impatient of submission, respected the

authority of the laws, and patiently supported the evils of
their social state, to which no one could apply a speedy
remedy.

If the Whig ministry had been as powerful in England
as it was in Ireland, if it could have commanded in the
House of Commons a majority strong enough to compel
the House of Lords to adopt the remedial measures
which it had prepared with a view to remove the
grievances of Ireland, all the wounds of that country
would have been on the way of cure, and political reforms
would gradually have brought about the social reforms
which alone could restore to Irish society the conditions of
repose and prosperity.

Fate decided otherwise. The Melbourne ministry instead of gaining, lost ground daily. Its moderate and
impartial policy towards Ireland did not suit the majority
in England. When Lord Stanley separated himself from
his colleagues, he told them truly: "I maintain confidently
that the country is not ripe for the Appropriation Bill,
and for the reform of the established church in Ireland."

Habits of oppression, rooted for centuries, are not
speedily overcome. Nations, like individuals, have difficulty in renouncing the ideas of superiority and of
domination which time has sanctioned. It must be long
before the whole English people can regard the Irish
as enjoying the same rights, and deserving the same
respect, as the proud descendants of the Saxons and the
Normans.

In spite of the sympathies of Ireland, the Melbourne
ministry—feebly supported by the Radicals, undermined
by the Chartists, violently attacked by the Tory party,
which, having gained strength in opposition, had been

reconstituted on a wider basis, under the name of the Conservative party—would not have long survived, had not Queen Victoria's accession to the throne given to it an auxiliary in the royal power. In its favour the Queen used her prerogatives to their furthest limits, and displayed in its support an energy and a firmness very remarkable at the outset of a reign begun at so early an age. Thanks to this help, Lord Melbourne was able to surmount more than one parliamentary storm, which endangered his ministerial existence; but, at last, he was forced to succumb before a decisive majority of the House of Commons.

The return of the Tories to power was a cruel blow to Ireland. In vain did Sir Robert Peel, in order to diminish its effect, seek among all his followers the wisest, the most conciliatory men, that he might confide to them the care of governing that country. The personal merits of the new Lord Lieutenant and of the new Secretary of State, Lord De Grey and Lord Elliot, could not prevent the discontent and irritation which the Irish could not but feel at the fall of the only government which had openly shown itself favourable to their cause. Very fortunately, nevertheless, the change of ministry having occurred against the wish of the Queen, and the Tories having been, so to speak, imposed by the majority of the Commons, the Irish, while they resumed their opposition, failed not to draw a just distinction between her person and her government. While they began anew a fierce struggle against her ministers, they preserved towards the Queen a very lively feeling of attachment and of gratitude, of which the agitation for the Repeal of the Union has not yet weakened the power.

In presence of a Tory ministry which commanded a numerous majority in both houses, O'Connell saw clearly that the cause of Ireland had nothing to expect from parliament. Mr. Peel, who had been restored to power by a Conservative and Protestant reaction, could grant nothing to the Catholics; it was even to be feared that his party might force upon him some violent measures, such, for example, as the bill on the formation of the electoral lists, which Lord Stanley had oftener than once submitted to the house when he was in opposition—a bill of which the effect would have been considerably to diminish the number of the electors. In order to prevent the adoption of retrograde measures, and to force the ministry to continue the work of justice which Lord Melbourne had begun, O'Connell, who had become powerless in parliament, had no resource but to revive the popular agitation, to begin anew the contest in the public street, and to reorganise a powerful association for the maintenance of his country's rights. He adopted it without hesitation. Quitting his place in the House of Commons he returned to Ireland, followed by almost all his Catholic colleagues; and resolute to resist, with all the arms that the British constitution affords to defeated parties, the projects of his adversaries. This determination was reasonable, if the question is judged from the Irish point of view; no one can blame O'Connell for having declined the parliamentary contest, in which his party were too much at disadvantage, and for having transported the strife to a ground on which he well knew that the prudent head of the government would not willingly meet him. It seems to me certain that, if he had continued this agitation within the bounds of the British constitution; if he had assigned to it an end pre-

cise and moderate ; if, for example, he had been content
with demanding the reform of the church, or the modification of the laws determining the relations between
landowners and their tenants,—he would most seriously
have embarrassed the Peel ministry, he would have effected
a speedy reaction in favour of his country in the public
opinion of Britain, and obtained, after a time, new concessions—a new victory. But this wise and prudent course
did not suit him. Either, intoxicated by past success, he
believed in the irresistible force of the means which he
was about to employ, or, more probably, thinking that, in
order strongly to stir the masses, to excite their passions,
and obtain from them an absolute devotedness, it was
necessary to hold out great objects to be accomplished, he
adopted an extreme course. Scarcely had he arrived in
Dublin, when he unfurled the banner of Repeal of the
Union, declaring that he would never withdraw from the
contest until he had obtained the re-establishment of his
country's national independence.

His powerful voice was heard from one end of Ireland
to the other. The sound awakened all the political and
religious passions, all the sentiments of nationality, which
during so many years he had been able to restrain. After
some months the whole Catholic population, and some
Protestants connected therewith, constituted an association more numerous, better organised, than that which
in 1829 wrested the Emancipation Bill from the Duke
of Wellington and Sir Robert Peel. This association
obeys its skilful leader with blind devotion. By its aid,
O'Connell at this hour wields a boundless empire over
seven-eighths of his countrymen; and the support of the
Catholic clergy tends to maintain and to extend his sway.

Up to the present time O'Connell has acted with great prudence. After having organised his army, he has passed in review its several corps, bringing together in different parts of the country all those who had enrolled themselves under the banner of Repeal. Was it the object of this display of force to intimidate England? Was this the prelude of more decisive measures? We know not. The prosecution which the government has thought fit to institute against him and his principal adherents has interrupted the course of those popular gatherings, and has not allowed him to complete the judicial organisation which he had devised in order to neutralise the influence of the legal magistracy; the same cause seems to have led him to postpone the project of bringing together the delegates from the different parts of the country, who were to form a sort of national assembly. Faithful to his system of peaceful opposition, he has bowed his head before the voice of law, and he has suspended the combat till after the decision of the jury before whom he is about to appear.

The union of so much audacity and so much prudence on the part of the Irish Catholics, of so much moderation and energy on the part of the English government, astonishes beyond measure the politicians of the continent, who have not a great knowledge of the principles on which rests the magnificent edifice of the British constitution. So long as the government remained inactive, they predicted a speedy revolution in Ireland, and its inevitable separation from the kingdom. Now, perhaps, struck with the feeble resistance offered to the first efforts of the ministry to repress the agitation and to arrest O'Connell in his course, they utterly despair of the cause of the Irish Catholics, and think them doomed to sterile contests, which can in no way improve their sad condition.

I do not hesitate to say that these two ways of judging the Irish question are equally erroneous. Some months ago, much undue importance was attached to the movement which O'Connell then so boldly directed ; we should be equally deceived if we failed to recognise the gravity of the dangers which it may threaten for the future. Ireland, covered with sores which centuries have envenomed, will be for a long time to come a source of embarrassment and of troubles to England. Even though the most prompt and efficacious remedies were applied, though all parties should agree in trying to effect a cure, its recovery could not for many years be complete ; more than one generation must pass away before all traces of discord and hatred, civil and religious, could be removed.

But such an agreement is not to be hoped for. Passions and prejudices are still too vigorous for England to be unanimous in regard to Ireland ; and this is but the smallest of the difficulties in the way of the regular development of that country. What in my eyes is more grave, is the severance which O'Connell has thought it right to make between his party and the whole British nation. Up to the present time the Irish Catholics had reckoned in England ardent and devoted partisans whose number was decidedly on the increase. By placing themselves above the oscillations of the policy of the day, it became easy to foresee the time when the friends of Ireland would have an irresistible majority in parliament. By displaying the banner of Repeal of the Union, O'Connell has broken with his old allies. He has placed himself face to face with England, and he has defied all its united strength. He has confounded in an equal enmity the Tories and the Whigs; the enemies of all reforms, of all concessions, and the most determined champions of civil and religious equality.

Europe, in general, has applauded the conduct of O'Connell, and has seemingly agreed with him in believing that the legislative independence of Ireland is the only effectual remedy for the evils of that country. Is this opinion well-founded? I am far from so thinking. On the contrary, I regard this notion as erroneous and as fatal to the improvement of the condition of the Irish people. In my opinion, O'Connell could not adopt a course more to be deplored. Instead of encouraging him to persist in it, the duty of all those who have at heart the interest of Ireland is to exhort him to retrace his steps, and to resume, along with the liberal British party, the work of progessive reform which he has already carried so far onward.

In proof of what I have now advanced, it is necessary, first, to examine the social state of Ireland, by searching out the true cause of the evils which she endures; next, to analyse the remedies which might be expected from a national legislature; and, lastly, to set forth the difficulties, the insurmountable obstacles in the way of the Repeal of the Union, and the numberless disadvantages which would attend the realisation of this project.

The task which I am about to undertake cannot completely solve the problem of the present state of Ireland, or pierce the darkness that hides the future reserved for it. It will serve at least, I hope, to throw some light on this interesting question, and to restrain within more reasonable limits the conjectures and the hypotheses to which it gives rise.

If the evils of Ireland could be imputed to its political state, she would need little pity, and their cure would be easy. In truth, she enjoys at this moment many more rights than most civilised nations whose lot is more prosperous. The press is there free even to license; individual liberty is religiously respected; the right of association is exercised to an extent nowhere else to be equalled; in a word, the Irish possess all the political rights of which the English are so justly proud. Do they, then, complain without reason? Are their sufferings imaginary? Alas! no. They are only too real. But in place of attributing them to political laws, we must seek their cause in the religious and social organisation of the country. Let us endeavour to explore the true principles on which this organisation rests.

Ireland, and especially Catholic Ireland, is a country exclusively agricultural. The cultivation of the ground is the chief—not to say the only—resource of the great majority of the population. This is ordinarily a condition eminently favourable to the maintenance of order and of peace; but here it is otherwise. The land, to which the Irish are attached by an insurmountable necessity, belongs almost wholly to a foreign race, which has for them neither sympathy nor affection, with which they are not united by the multitude of moral ties that everywhere else exist between the owner and the cultivator of the soil. The wars of invasion first, and religious strife afterwards, have several times transferred the property from the hands of the ancient possessors of the soil to those of the conquerors or the persecutors of the country. As a consequence of the successive confiscations which have taken place during the whole course of the seventeenth century,

E

Ireland, for a hundred years, has been divided into two hostile classes; one which possesses, the other which tills, the soil. Its population is composed of proprietors, Protestant, intolerant, haughty, treating with contempt those whom they have conquered; and of tenants, Catholic, poor, ignorant, superstitious, animated by an inveterate hatred of the despoilers of their country.

Such a social state has no parallel in Europe. Russia itself is, in this respect, in a more satisfactory condition. The serf, it is true, is legally in a state of absolute dependence on his master; he exercises fewer rights, he is subject to more of violent and arbitrary usage. But at least there exists between him and the upper classes of society a number of moral relations of which there is no trace in Ireland. The same blood flows in his veins and in those of his master; they worship at the same altars; they speak the same language; their national sympathies, their history, are the same; they have no remembrance of any change in their reciprocal positions. Nothing similar exists in Ireland. The Catholic cultivator regards the Protestant proprietors as cruel strangers who have robbed him of his goods; as sacrilegious persons who have profaned his holy temples; as enemies, in short, still stained with the blood of his forefathers. To form an idea of the state of misery and degradation into which the tyranny of William III. plunged Ireland, we must seek the terms of comparison in America—in the countries in which slavery still exists in all its hideousness.

These so hostile relations could not fail to disgust the proprietors with their domains as places of residence. The majority of them, in fact, caring very little to embellish or improve their estates, and pursued, besides, by a feeling of insecurity from which they cannot escape, think only of drawing from them the most money possible, without being obliged to make hazardous advances. The misery of Ireland raised up a class of grasping men who wonderfully strengthened these dispositions. These men, called "middlemen" *(entremetteurs)*, rented from the large proprietors who did not reside on their estates, a vast extent of badly cultivated land, unprovided with any sort of farm-buildings, or of the means of cultivation. Thereupon they divided the land into very small portions, and without even spending a farthing upon them to bring them into condition, they sub-let them to the wretched inhabitants of the country, among whom were often the descendants of the ancient proprietors who had been dispossessed by war and confiscations. This operation was often repeated; and the same domain passed into several hands, by division and sub-division, before coming to him who was finally to cultivate it; so that it is not rare, even at this day, to find between the proprietor and the true cultivator a hierarchy of five or six farmers, holding one from another.

This organisation of agricultural labour is, beyond contradiction, the worst that can exist. It unites to all the evils that can be charged upon the extreme division of the soil the vices of large properties; it renders impossible the division of labour, as well as improvements in agriculture, without redeeming its defects by the zeal, the activity, and the constant industry which the sentiment of property inspires.

The relative superiority of the two agricultural systems, of large and of small culture, will for a long time be a problem unsolved; but up to this time we may declare,

without fear of error, that the tillage of the soil consigned
to small farmers, without capital, without intelligence,
without affection for the soil they till, is the most deplorable kind of agriculture that it is possible to imagine.

Nevertheless as this agricultural system, however detestable, was eminently convenient to the proprietors, the
Irish parliament and the courts of justice did not cease to
favour it.   In order better to secure the payment of their
rents, the great landowners, who had at their disposal the
majority in the houses of parliament, passed a law which
rendered the farmer-cultivators responsible for what the
farmers intermediate between themselves and the proprietor might owe to him. Thus, a wretched peasant, after
having paid an exorbitant rent to the man who had let to
him the field on which he had so much difficulty to live,
was often called upon to pay the debts which the larger
farmers, to him unknown, had contracted with the proprietor of the soil.   This monstrous iniquity—this scandalous
abuse of power, which would of itself suffice to explain
the agrarian outrages which ever have been so frequent in
Ireland—subsisted even to 1830.   In that year, an Act,
known under the name of "The Sub-letting Act," declared
that every *bond fide* payment, made by a tenant to the
farmer from whom he held his land with the consent, expressed or tacit, of the proprietor, should be held as valid,
and could not be further questioned.

The selfish interests of the Irish landowners, who wished
above all things to be relieved from the care of their
estates, would have sufficed to extend throughout the
whole country the system of tenures just described; but
its extension was singularly favoured by causes foreign to
the organisation of property.   The first was the introduc-

tion of the potato, a plant eminently suited to the small culture. The second was that invincible tendency which, it cannot be denied, urges a poor, ignorant, brutalised population to increase its numbers as long as it can find means of subsistence, however wretched.

This is not the place to discuss Malthus' theory of population, and to establish within what limits it is true that population tends to increase in a proportion more rapid than the means of subsistence. I believe, with many modern economists, and especially Mr. Senior, who has treated this question with his usual ability, that the celebrated Malthus has exaggerated the effect of the *tendency* of the *force* which urges nations to multiply. Having had the very great merit of being the first to establish the universality of this tendency, it is not surprising that, dazzled by his own discovery, he has assigned to it a more considerable action than it really has. But whatever may be the general law which regulates the equilibrium of the forces which accelerate or retard the normal progress of the population, it is not doubtful that, in the particular circumstances of Ireland, the former must have exercised a preponderating influence.

When a people has fallen into a state of frightful misery,—when it has lost all hope of bettering its lot,—when the upper classes and the government do nothing to raise its moral condition,—it is evident that the powerful instinct which urges to reproduction will find no other obstacle than the want of subsistence. If, then, there be introduced into the country a system of agriculture which, like that of which the cultivation of the potato is the basis, is such as to make the soil produce a mass of alimentary substance detestable in quality, it is true, but, up to a

certain point, proportioned to the amount of labour applied
to it, the population will increase much more rapidly than
wealth, as long as there shall be fields to divide, and lands
capable of being subjected to the new mode of culture.

Mr. Senior, indeed, contests these theoretic conclusions.
He maintains that, in spite of the complaints raised on
all sides, the material condition of Ireland has improved
during the last fifty years. I cannot share his opinion:
testimonies the most irrefragable concur in disproof of it.
I will content myself, in order to prove what I have advanced, with quoting a few lines of the remarkable report
presented to parliament in 1839, by the commission which
had been appointed to inquire into the possibility and the
propriety of establishing railways in Ireland.

" We have perceived," say the Commissioners, " no symptom of
improvement in the condition of the people, who are almost exclusively wretched beings in rags, lodged in filthy cabins. In King's
County, as in all those that we have traversed, there is a frightful
excess of population. In a single barony, we have ascertained that
of 1,599 labourers, 668, or two fifths, are habitually without work."

Further on, the same Commissioners add :—

" Among the effects of this rapid increase of population, without
a corresponding increase of remunerative employment, the most
alarming, though perhaps the most obviously to be expected, is a
deterioration of the food of the peasantry. It could scarcely be
thought, indeed, that their customary diet would admit of any
reduction, save in quantity alone ; yet it has been reduced as to
quality also, in such a way as sensibly to diminish their comfort, if
not to impair their health. Bread was never an article of common
use amongst the labouring poor ; but it is now less known by them
than it was at the time when a sum exceeding £50,000 per annum
was paid in 'bounties,' to induce the landholders to grow a suffi-
ciency of grain for the supply of the city of Dublin. Milk is become
almost a luxury to many of them ; and the quality of their potato
diet is generally much inferior to what it was at the commencement
of the present century. A species of potato called the 'lumper' has

been brought into general cultivation, on account of its great productiveness, and the facility with which it can be raised from an inferior soil and with a comparatively small portion of manure. This root, at its first introduction, was scarcely considered food good enough for swine; it neither possesses the farinaceous qualities of the better varieties of the plant, nor is it as palatable as any other, being wet and tasteless, and, in point of substantial nutriment, little better, as an article of human food, than a Swedish turnip. In many counties of Leinster, and throughout the provinces of Munster and Connaught, the lumper now constitues the principal food of the labouring peasantry."

In the face of facts so decisive, it is impossible to accept the opinion of Mr. Senior; and we are forced to admit that the fatal system of sub-letting land in small portions, joined to other causes arising from the social circumstances of the country, has resulted in an increase at once of the population and of the misery and the suffering of the great mass of the people.

All the evils that I have pointed out are aggravated by the presence of a Protestant clergy who divide, with the rich proprietors, the fruit of the labour of the devotedly Catholic population in the midst of whom they live. This body of clergy has long been not only a continual cause of irritation, but even an occasion of scandal. The covetousness, the harshness, and the disorderly lives of the ecclesiastics of the Established Irish Church were in the last century proverbial. They are now greatly improved; and we now observe dispositions more humane, more charitable as well as more becoming lives. But not the less does the church remain, to the Catholics, the representative of the causes of their miseries, a sign of defeat and of oppression which exasperates their sufferings and makes their humiliation more keenly felt.

To complete the picture of the chief evils which have

afflicted the social life of Ireland, it suffices to add a few
words on the fatal effects of the spirit of disorder and of
vengeance which so great suffering has provoked among
the lower classes.   During nearly a century, Ireland
resounded with the reports of savage exploits, of abominable cruelties committed by associations of peasants,
who sometimes under the name of *Whiteboys*, sometimes
under that of *Whitefeet*, or under other designations, used
to avenge, often upon innocent persons, the outrages on
humanity committed by the class of proprietors and their
pitiless agents the middlemen.

These agrarian outbreaks, these servile wars, increased
all the evils of the country without abating any. If they
had continued with their primitive violence, the future of
the country would have been hopeless, and all idea of improving its condition must have been abandoned. Thanks
to Heaven, however, for some years Ireland has been deli-
vered from the scourge of this popular justice. The illegal
associations, energetically resisted by the leaders of the
Catholic party, have almost completely disappeared. This
is a symptom of moral progress that we may hail with joy
as the dawn of better days for the country.

After having pointed out the evils of Ireland, we must
inquire what has been done up to this time by way of
remedy. During the whole of last century the whole
business of the Irish parliament was to keep the Catholic
masses in check, without a single thought of improving
their condition. The parliament of the United Kingdom
pursued the same course during the first years that followed the Union. Protestant prejudices and national
antipathies did not allow the Catholics to be regarded
otherwise than as brutes, condemned to till the soil to

which they were bound for the exclusive benefit of the privileged classes. Nevertheless, when ideas of political reform and of religious tolerance had been diffused throughout England,—when the Catholic Association had revealed the extent of the means and intelligence possessed by the Irish who had remained faithful to their ancient worship,—every enlightened man in Great Britain began to occupy himself with the state of Ireland, and to take thought for the means of improving it. The parliament ordered several inquiries to ascertain the state of the country and to discover the source of its evils. In consequence of those inquires, it adopted in succession several remedial measures, the more important of which I will briefly recount.

In the first place it endeavoured to put an end to that fatal system of subdivision of the land, of which I have already indicated the dangerous results; and for this end it passed "The Sub-letting Act," of which I have before spoken. This measure was excellent in itself, and its happy consequences have already appeared. To it must be ascribed, in great measure, the diminution, during the last ten years, in the increase of the population, a fact to which public attention has been called by the last census. Nevertheless, through an unfortunate neglect, in providing for the future, no care was taken to secure the present lot of the miserable small tenants whom a vicious legislation had called into being, and great sufferings and great disorders were caused by this bill. A certain number of landowners, no longer finding in the system of sub-letting the security which they desired, evicted in mass the poor families who cultivated the ground under no other title than that of yearly tenants. These wretched people,

without resource, without shelter, often perished through
want or were compelled to seek beyond the seas a new
country, less cruel to them than that which had given
them birth.

The abolition of the tax for the repair of the churches,
the suppression of several bishoprics and other ecclesiastical benefices, the commutation of the tithes into
a direct charge on the landowners, were beneficent
acts, which sensibly ameliorated the religious state of
Ireland.

But of all that has been done within fourteen years for
the country, the measure which must effect the greatest
good, that which is destined in the fulness of time to effect
the moral regeneration of the people, is, beyond contradiction, the establishment of a vast system of popular education upon a wide and solid basis. The Whig ministry,
convinced that the only means of raising the lower classes
from the sad state in which they vegetated rather than
lived, was to develop their intelligence and to spread some
knowledge among them, resolved to found a great number
of primary schools with the sole object of instructing the
children who should frequent them, all attempt at religious
proselytism being forbidden. Some efforts had already
been made to diffuse popular instruction. A society, aided
by government, had long existed in Dublin, and from the
name of the street in which its meetings were held it had
received the title of the "Kildare Street Society." The
intentions of its founders were laudable; but, as, with
much zeal for education, they had also an ardent spirit of
Protestant proselytism, their efforts had but small success.
The Catholics regarded their schools with distrust, and in
general held themselves aloof.

The system of national education founded by the Whig ministry is different. All sectarian and proselytising spirit has been carefully banished from it. Its object is to diffuse instruction and morality, without doing any thing, directly or indirectly, to influence the religious faith of the children. Theological instruction is quite foreign to the mission of the schoolmasters; it is, nevertheless, obligatory on the pupils, but the duty of imparting it is confided wholly to the ministers of the religion professed by the parents. To secure the maintenance of this principle of religious impartiality, the administration of all these schools has been placed under the direction of a commission composed of Catholic prelates, of Protestant prelates, and of laymen of both bodies, as distinguished by their intelligence as by their tolerant spirit.

The success of this new plan of education has been complete. The Catholics have accepted it eagerly, and they avail themselves of it zealously. In all respects the national schools deserve great praise. The spirit which guides them, the methods which they employ, the results which they produce, render them true model schools. They are infinitely superior to the English primary schools, and I doubt that there are in Europe many that equal them. Through their agency, it is certain that the generation now growing up in Ireland will enjoy the benefits of an education intellectual and moral, solid and extensive. There is in them a mighty germ of progress which time will develop, and which will produce abundance of fruit very unlike that which may be expected from the political agitation that has the Repeal of the Union for its object or its pretext.

Lastly, among the means tried for improving the condition of Ireland, I will cite the law which establishes a poor-rate and the English system of legal charity. I do not assert that this system is good in itself, or that it is peculiarly suitable to Ireland. The questions raised by legal charity are in my view the most difficult of all those connected with the progressive transformation of the old social order; they are far from being settled. Those who, relying on the example of England, think they can condemn it absolutely, commit a grave error; for, if legal charity has produced some pernicious results, it has had the merit of testifying boldly to the obligations which society acknowledges towards the humblest of its members, and of propounding a problem of beneficence to which we must hope the progress of civilisation will, sooner or later, furnish a satisfactory solution.

Whatever may be the practical results in Ireland of the new poor-law, it will not the less remain as a striking proof of the benevolent disposition of parliament towards the poor of that island, of the spirit of equity and justice which begins to animate the representatives of the British nation. Though, even, it should wholly fail in the object which its authors had in view, this law would not the less deserve to be cited with commendation as the first example of a law passed in the sole interest of the Catholic masses, and of a sacrifice in their favour imposed upon the Protestant landowners.

The remedial measures which I have briefly enumerated are but trivial in comparison with the profound evils which afflict Ireland. Besides, their effect cannot be speedy; only time can render them fruitful and efficacious. At this day, though there have been, especially during the last few years, partial amelioration and progress, the state of the great mass of the population is, nevertheless, deeply distressing. It is, then, natural that all the friends of humanity should feel an ardent interest in the remedies likely to bring a prompt relief.

Can it be that the first, the most important of those remedies, is the Repeal of the Legislative Union, which, for four and forty years, has existed between Britain and Ireland? Ought we to hope from Repeal the cure of the diseases of the Irish nation, which O'Connell every day proclaims amidst the applause of the enthusiastic multitude? Can it be true, as most of the continental politicians seem to think, that a parliament sitting in the hall of College Green at Dublin would have the power instantaneously to cure the social sores of Ireland, and to restore the social edifice on an equitable and beneficial basis, so as to develop among all classes a prosperity hitherto unknown? This is the great question of the moment; and it is important that it should be answered, in order that we may judge if the schemes of O'Connell and his party are reasonable and well founded,—if their purpose, which they cannot realise by force, has at least truth and justice on its side.

Let us, at the outset, try to form a precise idea of what O'Connell and the Irish Association understand by the Repeal of the Union. In the first place, the only question hitherto has been regarding legislative independence; not at all political independence. Queen Victoria has no subjects more devoted than the Irish Catholics, who, even while they demand a national parliament, wish to maintain intact upon her head the brilliant crown of the British Isles. This parliament, however, which they so eagerly

demand, cannot be the same as that which existed before
the Union. The Liberator would, assuredly, render a sorry
service to his country, and above all to his party, if he
tried to restore Ireland to the state in which she was in
1799. In spite of the illusions which the dazzling memories of the movement in 1782 may produce, it is easy to
learn that the majority of the Irish nation was then much
more oppressed, and that it had much more just reason
for complaint than it has now. The old Irish parliament,
I have already said, was an obedient instrument in the
hands of the cabinet of St. James'; it was serviceable
only to the owners of rotten boroughs—to the traders in
parliamentary influence, who openly sold the rights and
liberties of their fellow-citizens.

But, in spite of the regret which O'Connell sometimes
expresses, no one thinks of restoring the old Irish constitution. What the Association desires is the creation of a
national parliament on the bases which Catholic Emancipation and the Reform of 1832 have consecrated, in which
the Catholic and popular element should have an incontestable preponderance.

After so many centuries of dependence and submission,
the Catholic majority aspires to power and domination in
its turn.

Nevertheless, in order to disunite the kingdoms which
compose the British empire, it is not enough to declare
that the Irish representatives and peers, instead of meeting,
as now, at Westminster, shall meet on College Green, in
Dublin. The relations must be settled between the
executive power and houses of legislature in the two
countries; it would be necessary to divide between them
the powers which they exercised in common. Here

we see numberless difficulties arise, which neither O'Connell nor any other Irish orator has yet attempted to resolve.

If, in the British constitution, the functions of the parliament were purely administrative ; if, even, it did not extend beyond the sphere of legislation,—we might manage to understand the co-existence of two independent legislatures, sitting one in London, the other in Dublin. But everyone knows that in England the parliament has a preponderating influence on the executive power ; that foreign and colonial policy is subject to its control : that nothing of serious importance is done without its approval and its sanction. This being so, how can these high functions be divided between the legislators of the two countries ? How can their independent action be harmonised ? I do not think that it is possible to devise, for this end, any means that can resist a few moments' examination. In no country, and assuredly not in Great Britain, in which so many diverse interests claim an incessant care, can the executive power be subject to two distinct influences. A ministry obliged to please at once an English majority and an Irish majority, is a thing impossible. In contradiction to this view, we may, perhaps, be referred to the state of Great Britain from 1782 to the establishment of the Union, a period during which two parliaments nominally independent existed at London and at Dublin. But this argument is an illusion. Every one knows very well that the old Irish parliament was dependent on the English ministry, and that as soon as one party had the majority at Westminster, it was sure, by means of certain pecuniary sacrifices, absolutely to overrule the Irish parliament.

In order to prove the real independence of the Irish parliament, some obstinate disputants may still appeal to the dissension between it and the English parliament on occasion of the temporary regency of the Prince of Wales, at the time of the first illness of George III. We know, indeed, that on this occasion the English Houses, controlled by Pitt, refused to grant more than a very limited power to the hereditary prince; while the Irish Houses, in spite of all the efforts of ministerial agents, persisted in investing him with all the powers of royalty. The fact is indubitable, but, in my opinion, it is far from proving the independence of the Irish parliament. It is but one more indication of its servile instinct, which sought, by dangerous concessions, to propitiate the regent into whose hands supreme power, sooner or later, was to fall. It is impossible honestly to contend that, with an independent legislature, Ireland can continue to exert the slightest influence on foreign or colonial policy. This is the first sacrifice which the Repeal of the Union would impose upon the country. Has the Liberator well considered its importance? Has he thought how humiliating it would be for his country to follow in the political orbit the powerful star of Great Britain, without being able in any way to influence its course? Has he thought how injurious it would be to his country to renounce all political connection with the immense colonies of England, the vast regions which are as necessary to it for the reception of its surplus population, as they are useful to Great Britain in receiving the overflow of its manufactures?

For my part, I am convinced that the Irish nation has too much pride and dignity ever to submit to hold a position so dependent and secondary as that to which the division of the two kingdoms would reduce it, even though at this price an independent parliament should be obtained.

Some persons have thought that all interests could be reconciled by placing above the two parliaments a third and supreme assembly, with the sole duty of deciding questions of foreign and colonial policy. Possessed by this idea, Mr. Sharman Crawford, who represents the opinion of the Protestant Radicals, offered some time ago to the Liberator to co-operate with him, if he would consent to modify his schemes of absolute independence, and to substitute for them a sort of Anglo-Hibernian confederation. It is easy to see that this plan is still more difficult of execution than those which we have already examined. In fact, how is it possible to reconcile the action of three legislative assemblies, and of three executive powers, which must be, within certain limits, independent of each other. In a country which has with other countries so numerous relations, there is scarcely any measure of foreign or colonial policy which does not directly influence its home policy. When war is declared, taxes must be imposed; when treaties of commerce are made, modifications of the customs tariff are indispensable; many treaties involve changes in the civil law. How, then, could an Anglo-Irish congress carry its ordinances into effect by means of parliaments almost as powerful as itself? It would be impossible. The representative machine, already so complicated and so slow, could not work after its springs had been tripled, after three parliaments had been established instead of one. All the energy of Pitt, all the genius of Canning, would be

F

incompetent to work it; they would be forced to abandon the direction and the defence of interests so great and so various as those which connect Great Britain with almost every place on the globe.

The example of the Swiss or the American confederation cannot be cited as a proof of the possibility of establishing an Anglo-Hibernian confederation; first, because the foreign affairs of those countries are as simple, and as few in number as those of Britain are important, numerous, and complex; secondly, because they have not numerous colonies to maintain in a position of semi-dependence as delicate as it is difficult; because they have not an empire of a hundred million of inhabitants, like that of India, to govern; lastly, because the United States have no continental neighbours to fear, while Switzerland is relatively too weak to exert any positive action on the great powers that surround it. It is, besides, impossible to liken a confederation formed by a great number of states, among which no one is much stronger than several others united, to the confederation which it may have been wished to establish between the British colossus and Ireland which is so inferior to it in strength and power. It is obvious that, in a numerous confederation, the interests of the different states are balanced and grouped in a manner favourable to the states so united. But in a case in which two nations only should be face to face, the weaker would always follow the law of the stronger. Any such congress would serve only to make known to Ireland the commands of England.

If we view the question on all its sides, we shall be convinced that, were the Union dissolved, Britain must

either resolve to hold Ireland in a state of subjection and
dependence worse than that which now exists, or leave
her to follow freely the course of her destinies; and, in
this case, the words of Sir Robert Peel may be adopted,—
that "to retain Ireland after the Repeal of the Union in
a course accordant with that of the British empire, would
require not less than the omniscience and the omnipotence
of the Supreme Being who maintains the harmony of the
planetary system."

But let us pass over all the difficulties which the
Repeal of the Union might cause in regard to foreign
and colonial policy; let us suppose them removed by a
miracle of Divine Providence, and let us inquire if the
benefits which Ireland may hope from a national government are as considerable as the Liberator and his
partisans assert. At the first glance it seems probable
that the finances of Ireland would be improved by the
Repeal of the Union. Those who accept literally the
declarations of O'Connell must be supposed to think
that the country bears a part of the public burdens
disproportioned to its population and its wealth; that
it would consequently be much relieved, if it had to
provide only for its own wants by its own resources.
This is, however, a complete illusion. Ireland has not
been unjustly treated in a financial respect; if left to
itself, it would probably be obliged to increase its present
taxes, if not to impose new. Let us see what it really
pays.

The Union had placed at its charge two-seventeenths
of the expenses of the United Kingdom. This is a division, if not favourable, at least equitable. Since that time

its share has diminished.   In an official document, published in 1834, we find the following distribution of the
produce of the imposts in the two kingdoms :—

	GREAT BRITAIN.	IRELAND.
Customs	£19,353,324	... £1,757,143*
Excise...............	13,061,852	... 1,966,183
Post	1,970,361	... 240,471
Stamps	6,825,679	... 466,170
Taxes	4,662,256	... —
Total	£45,873,472	... £4,429,967

From this it follows that Ireland bears an eleventh
part of the public burdens, which is much less than that
which the Act of Union assigned.

It will be remarked that the impost known under the
name of taxes appears in the column of Ireland, followed
only by a blank.   The fact is, that since 1825 it has been
abolished in Ireland, while it still subsists in England.

Since the year to which the figures just cited refer,
Great Britain, having been involved in extraordinary
expenses on account of the affairs of Canada and the
Chinese expedition, has been compelled to draw fresh
resources from taxation.   Sir Robert Peel had the courage
to propose and to carry through parliament a tax on

---

* It is necessary to observe that a part of the foreign merchandise subject to customs duty, which Ireland consumes, is imported from England,
after having paid duty there.   In order, therefore, to make a rigorous
comparison between the burdens of the two countries, we must take into
account the sum yielded by those duties.   This would require very complicated investigations ; according, however, to calculations which may be
regarded as sufficiently exact, we may reckon them approximately at
£5,000,000. This increase would modify the proportion given above, and
raise to a tenth the share of the public burdens that falls upon Ireland.

incomes; but, in consideration of the position of Ireland, he exempted that country from it. Thus, at this time, the proportion before shown has been further modified in favour of that country.

These incontestable facts suffice to absolve Britain from the charge of having abused its strength in order to crush Ireland with taxation; they show, on the contrary, that in matters of finance Ireland has been generously treated.

Let us now inquire what would be the position of Ireland if left to herself. If we suppose that no change be made in existing imposts, she might, according to the table before given, dispose of a revenue of £4,429,967, which sum, to be more exact, I will raise to £5,000,000, in order to allow for goods which she consumes but which now pay customs dues in England. From these £5,000,000 must first be paid the interest of the portion of the debt of the United Kingdom which will remain chargeable to Ireland; for, even if disunited, she must still retain a part of the burden now borne by her in common with England. O'Connell never ceases to compare the amount of the Irish debt with that of the British debt at the time of the Union, to prove the wrong which, he says, has been done to his country. I suppose that there is a full intention to repair this wrong, and that, consequently, the obligation to contribute to the payment of old debts is abolished. By old debts I mean those contracted before the beginning of the war of the French revolution; this would be a basis not only equitable, but still favourable to Ireland; for in truth she had an old debt, and it would have been but reasonable to require, while sharing with her the advantages which the vast colonies of Great Britain secured to the mother country, that she should contribute to the costs which, in the conquest of these, the country had incurred. To ask more would be ridiculous and absurd. The Liberator himself cannot entertain the thought, unless he think that one day, at the head of a victorious army, he will be able to dictate laws to conquered Britain.

On this principle, Britain alone would be charged with £239,350,148, which she owed in 1783. The rest of the public debt, including the exchequer bills, rose in 1836 to £787,638,816. There would then remain to be divided between the two countries a debt of £548,288,668. By charging Ireland with £60,000,000, no injustice would be committed; impartial arbiters would treat her more severely. That sum of £60,000,000 of debt would cost about £2,000,000 in interest, and this would reduce the part of her revenue available for public service to £3,000,000 (*i. e.* 75,000,000 of francs). This is a very scanty revenue for a country of eight millions of inhabitants. All the states of Europe spend in proportion to their population twice, thrice, even six times more than this. It would be wholly insufficient, to enable Ireland to dispose of any military force, and to maintain the police and the magistracy on the footing on which they are at present constituted. One of the first consequences of Repeal, accordingly, would be to force upon the parliament of Dublin an increased taxation.

But, it will be said, it is not the amount of imposts which makes Ireland suffer; it is the manner in which they are distributed. It is enough to inquire what are the chief sources of the public revenues, in order to be convinced that the state-burdens fall almost exclusively on the rich classes, or on the vicious part of the population.

The customs form nearly half of the resources of the state. Now these consist almost wholly of the duties on colonial products, sugar and tea in particular. By reduction of those duties, the middle class would probably be relieved; but six-sevenths of the population would find not the least benefit, for these articles do not at all enter into their consumption.

With the customs, the excise forms almost the whole of the public revenue of Ireland; now it is well known that it is the duties on the manufacture of spirits that constitute four-fifths of this branch of revenue, and no one, so far as I am aware, thinks of demanding their reduction.

It is certain, therefore, that the Repeal of the Union could not make any beneficial change either in the amount of taxes, or in the manner in which they are levied. But the evils of Ireland are not caused by financial abuses; it signifies little, therefore, that a national government should be unable to make improvements in this respect, if it could lay its hand on their true source, and effect a thorough change in the deplorable social and religious condition of the country.

I have already spoken of the organic vices of Irish society. These may be summed up under two distinct heads: first, the supremacy of a worship odious to the majority of the population; secondly, the deplorable state to which the agricultural population are reduced, by the bad distribution of property, by the feelings of hostility which separate the different classes of society; and lastly, by the effects of a too rapid growth of the poor population. Let us see what a national parliament could do by way of remedy to these.

We must begin by forming an idea of what the Irish
parliament would be, of the spirit which would animate
it, and of the parties that in it would arise. It is evident
that, if Repeal were obtained, it would be due to the successful efforts of the popular and Catholic party, and, consequently, that the first independent legislature would
consist almost wholly of members of that party. What
else, indeed, could the Protestants expect or hope ? The
destruction of the municipal corporations has secured the
majority to the Catholics in all the towns, and the right of
voting possessed by all the farmers paying £10 sterling
in rent, guarantees their triumph in four-fifths of the
counties, as often as a great national interest is involved.
It is no exaggeration, therefore, to assert that three-
fourths of the House of Commons, owing its existence to
Repeal, would be Catholic democrats.

Their treatment of the Anglican Church would not be
doubtful. They would reform it, or, to speak more truly,
they would destroy it utterly. O'Connell declares that
the rights of existing holders of ecclesiastical benefices
would be respected. Of this I have strong doubts. The
Catholics, intoxicated with the success of their long
efforts, would not act with so scrupulous delicacy towards
a clergy whom they regard as the primary cause of the
humiliations and the sufferings which their fellow reli-
gionists have endured for ages. The protestations of
O'Connell inspire me with little confidence; constant as
he is to the object at which he aims, he does not at all
hesitate to vary his means, and to repudiate the engage-
ments which hamper him, forgetting to-morrow the promises of to-day. For my part, I will think the Protestant
ecclesiastics very fortunate if, after Repeal, the revolution

be effected simply by legal measures, and without such treatment by the masses as was a few years ago, in Spain, experienced by the convents.

Nevertheless, the reform of the established church is so essential to the well-being of Ireland, that we must not regard too strictly the means employed to effect it. I do not hesitate to declare that, if the Repeal of the Union were indispensable to this end, I could not but desire it, in spite of all the evils which this measure must involve. But happily this necessity does not exist. The Radical reform of the church not only is possible without the Repeal of the Union, but it is even probable, if the violent acts of the Catholic party do not arrest the movement of English public opinion in its favour. The Whigs attempted this reform; their attempt was premature, and it did not succeed. But they have not abandoned their task; on the contrary, the men who are the hope of this party for the future are much more daring now than they were in 1835; and, in my judgment, we have a certain symptom of the downfall, sooner or later, of the *establishment* in Ireland, in the fact that a member of such standing as Mr. Ward, with the concurrence of a numerous party, this year presented to parliament a motion which aimed at nothing less than the suppression by a single stroke of the pen of the whole factitious edifice of the state religion in Ireland. The reform of the established church will come to pass, in one way or other. With a national parliament it would be more speedy and more complete; but it would probably be also violent, unjust, and perhaps cruel. If the Union continue, it will be effected slowly by regular and legal means. I can understand a preference of the former course; but whatever love of revolutions there may be, we cannot forget how costly to humanity are the sudden and violent derangements which always follow in their train.

The religious question furnishes plausible arguments to the partisans of Repeal. The case is different with the social question. This, at least, is the inevitable result of a thorough analysis of the remedial measures which a national parliament might adopt, and a conscientious comparison of them with those which have been, and with those which probably will be adopted by the reformed parliament, if no violent shocks occur.

To raise the peasant class from their present sad condition, there are two sorts of remedies: we may endeavour to improve their lot by regular legal and pacific means; or, adopting a bolder system, we may seek to destroy the evil at its root, by violently changing the laws which determine the distribution of property; by at once freeing the tenant from his dependence on his landlord; by effecting, to speak clearly, a true social revolution, which should restore to the present Catholic population the lands of which their ancestors were despoiled by civil wars and by repeated confiscations.

The former system may be applied more or less successfully, either by an Irish parliament, or by the parliament such as it is now. The latter is impossible, unless the Repeal of the Union—or more strictly, the absolute isolation of Ireland—should leave to the popular party a free field of action. I decline to discuss their comparative merits, not because I think there is no one who prefers the more violent course; on the contrary, I believe that it is preferred by all extreme parties, by all the enemies of Great Britain, whether democratic or aristocratic. For widely different reasons, indeed, both parties would rejoice to see that country a prey to revolutionary storms : the Radicals, because such is their natural bent ; the enemies of progress, because they bitterly hate Britain, which in their eyes is, as it were, the fatal workshop in which are elaborated in safety all ideas subversive of the ancient order of things, and from which they are sent forth to conquer the world. But, as I have no intention to address these extreme parties, I think it useless to stop to examine a system which, whatever may be its final results, is founded on injustice and proscriptions, on violations of moral law and of humanity.

While, then, I regard solely legal and peaceful means, I will examine in succession the chief measures which can improve the state of the Irish masses. These may be ranged under five heads, according as they have for their object popular education, commerce and industry, great works of public utility, the organisation of public relief and emigration ; lastly, the amendment of the civil laws affecting the distribution of property and the relations of the landowners and their tenants. We shall discuss in order each of these categories.

I. POPULAR INSTRUCTION.—Education is the first necessity of Ireland. That only can raise the morals and enlighten the intellect of the masses brutalised by ages of oppression and misery. That only, by developing among the people a sentiment of prudence, can arrest the pernicious increase of the population, and establish a less lamentable proportion between the number of inhabitants and their means of subsistence. The Irish have a lively intelligence ; they seek instruction eagerly, and they learn quickly. It is almost true to say that the best government for Ireland will be that which will diffuse most light among the poorer classes, and do most to dispel the darkness of dense ignorance in which they have vegetated hitherto.

I have already spoken of the laudable efforts of the Whig ministry to found a vast system of national education, on a plan eminently tolerant and reasonable. That plan, which has been received with favour and sympathy by the Catholics, has succeeded beyond the hopes of its founders. The national schools have multiplied rapidly, and their number, already very considerable, is daily on the increase. The good which they do is immense, for they are conducted on a system, and by methods which leave nothing to be wished by the most exacting advocates of popular instruction. Thanks to the establishment of normal schools, which are true models, the day is not distant when there shall be established in every part of Ireland primary schools to satisfy the intellectual needs of the population. The future of this great work has not been endangered by the accession of the Conservative party to power. At the outset, the fanatical partisans of the established church attacked it violently, and all the energy of the Melbourne ministry was required to maintain progress in the course on which it had entered. But now the benefits of the national schools are so great and so universally recognised, that Sir Robert Peel will do all in their favour that Lord John Russell could have done.

Would a national parliament hasten this intellectual movement? It may well be doubted. The existing system is based on the complete absence of proselytism, on a spirit of absolute impartiality among the different religious creeds. The men who direct it are justly reputed as the most intelligent, the wisest, and most moderate of the clergy—Catholic and Protestant—along with the most eminent laymen of the country. Would it remain unchanged if power were to pass into the hands of the Catholic democracy? Assuredly not. It would certainly be disposed to place under the sole direction of the clergy the national schools,—all those at least which exist in the provinces, where the Protestants are an imperceptible minority. Such a result will be regarded as certain by all those who, relying on the lessons of history, reflect on the tendencies of religious parties when they have all political power in their own hands. Now this would be a great misfortune to the country, an obstacle to the progress of instruction.

No one is more disposed than I to render justice to the Catholic clergy. I honour their sincere faith, their zealous charity, their boundless self-devotion ; but I do not recognise in them the qualities necessary to direct successfully popular instruction. Their profound ignorance, their numerous prejudices, their exaggerated political notions, render them unfit to fulfil the mission which the primary teacher ought to propose to himself—to develop the intelligence and to raise the moral dignity of childhood. If the national schools were entrusted to the clergy they would soon fall, from the high degree of perfection which they have attained, to the level of the Belgian schools. The instruction would cease to be intelligent, and the lower classes would derive much less benefit from them.

As the merits of the present system cannot be gainsaid, it will perhaps be alleged that an Irish parliament, would devote to popular instruction a much larger annual sum than that which is now granted. This is possible.

But it is equally true that, if the popular party were to demand the increase of this sum with a hundredth part of the zeal displayed in the pursuit of an impossibility, they would obtain from parliament, whatever party might occupy the Treasury benches, more money than is required to found schools in every parish.

II. COMMERCE AND INDUSTRY.—What have these to hope from the legislative independence of Ireland ? What means could the Irish government have for rapidly developing these two principal sources of the prosperity of nations? In this respect, I confess my complete ignorance. Some persons think, perhaps, that by adopting a protective system, by closing its ports to Britain, Ireland could make many branches of manufacture flourish at home. Nothing more absurd can be imagined. A war of tariffs between the two islands would be pernicious to both ; but Britain would suffer much less than Ireland. Ireland, essentially by nature agricultural, finds in Great Britain the most advantageous market in the world for the sale of its products. Even if we suppose that the condition of the lower classes is improved as is to be desired, even if those classes were able to consume a much larger amount of articles of food, Ireland will always yield (however little its agriculture may share in the general improvement which we suppose) a surplus of agricultural produce, which it must export. If England close her ports against her, what will she do with her butter, her corn, her wheat ? Driven to sell them at a loss on the continent, she will see her agriculture reduced to terrible distress.

Britain, on the other hand, would lose little by exchanging her manufactured goods for the grain of Canada and of the Baltic, for the butter of Holland, instead of exchanging them, as now, for the produce of Ireland; and if she had to bear some losses, these would be, in any case, much less than those of her rival. It is, then, quite clear that to establish fiscal barriers between Ireland and Britain would be an act of madness.

It is, besides, certain that Ireland cannot aspire, at present, to become an industrial power. There are wanting the elements necessary for the development of industry: capital and the chief kinds of raw material. The Repeal of the Union would not give her either the iron or the coal which would be necessary; and still less would it increase the mass of capital needful for a great development of industry. By the aid of bounties, of privileges, and of other costly encouragements, a factitious industry might perhaps be introduced into Ireland; but such a result, far from being desirable, would be to be dreaded as a new means of aggravating, sooner or later, the distress of the working classes.

III. PUBLIC WORKS.—Of all the measures hitherto proposed, that which would give to Ireland if not the most complete, at all events the most speedy, relief, is the execution of vast public works of a kind to employ a part of the labour not required by agriculture. The Irish, if well paid and well fed, are eminently qualified for labour which requires great muscular strength. They are excellent labourers. The French people have had means of judging, by the way in which the men laboured whom the contractors for the Paris and Rouen railway had brought over from the other side of the Channel, and who were almost all Irish. Consequently, the execution of such enterprises as canals, harbours, railways, would be favourably conducted in Ireland, since manual labour, which constitutes the chief cost of similar works, is there abundant and cheap.   But an available working population is not the only condition needful for the accomplishment of the enterprises just mentioned.   To set that population in motion, there are needed the sinews of all things—money, capital.   To procure these is the great difficulty.   Would it be less when Ireland had obtained an independent legislature?   I cannot think so.   For whether the execution were undertaken by private companies, or by the government itself, capital would be less disposed than now to seek employment in Ireland.   The country itself possesses little ; if it wish to undertake great works, it must have recourse to British capitalists.   Those, who already hesitate to invest their money on the other side of the St. George's Channel, would probably refuse altogether to risk it in a country which had become to them a quite foreign land. For a long time, if Repeal were effected, the Protestant coins of London would distrust the good faith of the democratic parliament of Dublin.   It is, then, probable that this measure would retard, rather than advance, the execution of the public works which the interests of Ireland imperiously demand.

If, on the contrary, the Union be maintained,—if the feverish agitation of Repeal be calmed,—it is certain that the government will resume the projects already suggested under the Melbourne ministry, and that it will provide Ireland with a network of railways like that which covers Great Britain.   Sir Robert Peel has already declared that if he opposed the schemes of his predecessors in office, it was only because he preferred to leave the field open to private industry; but that this not having fulfilled his expectation, he was disposed to return to his first thoughts.

From this declaration, I should be inclined to think that, in the next session, the ministry will do something for Irish railways. May God inspire them with a determination, noble, comprehensive, energetic, worthy of the great nation which they govern, and lead them to adopt a plan which, embracing the whole country, may produce, in some measure, a happy revolution in the rate of wages!*

Railways, independently of the temporary advantages which they would yield by creating a vast demand for labour, would singularly advance the work of regeneration which popular instruction is called on to accomplish. By destroying distances, by placing, so to speak, wild Connaught at the gate of Dublin; by bringing nearer together the inhabitants of all parts of the island, by furnishing them with the occasion and the means of seeing and of knowing each other, they would contribute to weaken

* In the Memoir of Thomas Drummond, by John F. Mc.Lennan, Edin., 1867, c. xvii., pp. 341—401, there is a full and most interesting account of the Report of the Commission on Irish Railroads appointed in October, 1836, and of the hostility and indifference that proved fatal to its recommendations. After the lapse, and, in part, the loss, of more than thirty years, another Commission is now considering the subject of Irish railways. Its secretary is Dr. Hancock, a sound economist and an indefatigable statist, whose striking observations on the Financial Condition of Irish Railways are quoted by Mr. Mc.Lennan in Appendix No. VII., p. 464. Mr. Mc.Lennan says, in words as sad as they are just: "Mr. Drummond's benevolent scheme for the improvement of the masses of the Irish was destined to be thwarted through British selfishness and obtuseness. Its results, at least, were lost when, by his untimely death, the genius that had conceived and directed the project was withdrawn. Some of those who were foremost in opposing him are now, I am assured, the most clamorous for the purchase of the Irish railways by the state. It is the old story— the good that might have been done can only be conjectured—the evil that might have been averted we must suffer as best we may."—p. 397.—*Translator.*

G

those prejudices of race, those antipathies of sect, which have wrought so much evil to the country.

Lastly, railways would give to Ireland great commercial importance. 'If one of those marvellous lines crossed the island from east to west, placing St. George's Channel in prompt communication with the western shore washed by the Atlantic; if the distance which separates the walls of Dublin from the harbours of Connaught could be traversed in eight hours, Ireland would of necessity become the highway between the two hemispheres: its future would be magnificent. The consequences of such an enterprise would be immense, not only for Ireland, but for the whole world. Trans-Atlantic navigation, having its point of departure on the furthest shores of County Clare, rendered thus more easy and less costly, would be prodigiously extended. Imagine what, in a not distant future, would be the relations of America and Europe, if in seven days' time men could pass from one hemisphere to the other.

If the British nation speedily accomplish a work which must have results so magnificent, it will have done much to repair the wrongs which its ancestors have inflicted upon Ireland, and to fill up the gulph which the hatreds of ages have dug between the two islands so near in space, so far off in feeling.

IV. EMIGRATION: POOR-RATES.—A system of well managed legal aid, supported by emigration on a great scale, would, doubtless, give substantial relief to the labouring class employed in agriculture. By forcing, on one hand, the landowners to take an interest in the lot of the poor of their parish, and, on the other, by diminishing the number of the unhappy people who now compete so terribly for a morsel of land to cultivate, or for insufficient wages, it would necessarily produce a rise in wages, and a fall in the rents of small pieces of land.

If these measures were accompanied by the extension to all parts of Ireland of the present system of education ; if the government, the clergy, and the upper classes, employing all the means of influence and of action which society has at its disposal, were to vie with each other in the effort to develop the intelligence and to raise the morals of the lower classes, a permanent amelioration would ensue. The Irish workmen, better instructed and less ignorant, would become more provident, and, after having been lifted from the wretched mire in which they have so long vegetated, they would strive to go on mounting the steps of the social ladder, and to attain a more prosperous state than that of the agricultural populations of either Britain or the continent.

The efficacy of such remedies being admitted, it follows that the Repeal of the Union would be a great good, if it were certain that an Irish legislature would endeavour to apply them with energy and success. But it is easy to see that a purely Irish parliament would not inevitably take so rational a course. The popular party has in all times shown the most intense repugnance to the principle of legal charity as it is understood in Great Britain.

When the Melbourne ministry attempted to introduce into Ireland the system of poor-rates, O'Connell opposed it with his accustomed violence. He has since resisted its application by all the means in his power. It is, then, reasonable to think that, if the government of Ireland were to fall into his hands, one of his first cares would be to suppress the poor-rate, and to destroy all that has been done to apply to the country the English system of legal charity.

The expedient of emigration would be more to the taste of the popular party. The Irish parliament would not oppose it; but if it had recourse to it, it would find almost insurmountable difficulties in its execution. All the efforts of statesmen, and all the plans, more or less ingenious, of economists, have failed to resolve the problem of transporting, without an enormous cost, great numbers of men and women across the ocean. The colonies in which it is still possible to secure a happy existence for a large number of emigrants, are the most distant. Canada is in danger of being overcrowded by a population purely of the lower classes; already the last immigrants have found there a competition as keen as that from which they fled when they quitted Europe.

There are only the vast continents of Oceania open to receive and able usefully to employ the waves of emigration. It is unfortunate, for the cost of transporting a family from Ireland to New Holland is the double of that required for a passage to Canada.

The fact being so, how could Ireland, if abandoned to her own resources, undertake a vast plan of emigration? In this case also, much more than in the question of railways, would the want of capital make her powerless. Besides, if even she could find the means of procuring it, she must have recourse to England and entreat her to receive the surplus of the population; she would be compelled to humble herself before the haughty rival against whom she had sustained so fierce a struggle. If she consented to do this, I do not see what would be the benefit of the Repeal of the Union. Assuredly, this measure would not tend to raise the moral dignity of the country.

V. REFORM OF THE LAWS OF TERRITORIAL PROPERTY.—The inquiry now made regarding the first four measures that we have viewed as the only possible remedies for the evils of Ireland tends also to prove that the Repeal of the Union, far from facilitating their application, would render it difficult and dangerous. It remains for me to examine the last question, the most important of all, that is, what could be done to bring about a better distribution of property in land, and to improve the relations between the proprietors and the tenants ?

Let me repeat, at the outset, that we have excluded from the discussion every scheme based on spoliation and revolution. We must assume as our foundation that the Irish parliament would respect vested rights, and that it would renounce the seductive but guilty thought of avenging on the present generation the crimes of past generations, and would content itself with regulating and modifying, without violently destroying, the now existing rights of property. Within the circle so restricted, there would still be much to do.

M. de Beaumont, in his remarkable work on Ireland, has very well shown that almost all the evils which afflict the country may be referred to the existence of a bad aristocracy. It is evident, in fact, that in a country where property in land is the source of almost all powers, the most pernicious of things possible is that the class of proprietors and the other classes who form the great mass of society should belong to races and to religions opposed, rivals, hostile to each other. Here is, I cannot repeat it too often, the fatal germ of an infinitude of evils which corrupt and vitiate all the political and social institutions of the country. Nothing, consequently, can be done more useful to Ireland than to try to change this vicious state, by substituting for the existing class of Protestant proprietors, Catholic proprietors, who should inspire the masses of the people with sympathy in all their relations.

By the "pure and simple" confiscation of the property of Protestants, by their forced sale, and by other measures of this kind, an assembly such as the French National Convention would speedily attain this end; but these abominable expedients revolt all honest minds. It is for us, then, to see what can be hoped from a modification of the civil laws which relate to the right of property.

The laws which regulate the transmission and the distribution of landed property in Ireland, are analogous to those of Great Britain. Their chief object is to maintain the possession of it without change or partition, in the same families, and to prevent its being broken up into small portions by successive divisions. I do not wish to discuss their absolute merit; in their favour numerous arguments may be alleged, and the example of England gives to these great weight. But, however advantageous they may be to a society organised wholly in accordance with their principle, it cannot be denied that in Ireland their sad effect is to maintain a deplorable state of things. Reform, then, would be desirable, for the greatest admiration of the aristocratic system cannot disguise the fact that the greatest services that could be rendered to that country would be to deliver it from its Protestant aristocracy, as a preliminary for creating another aristocracy which should be Catholic.

If the civil law did not check the transferrence of properties, this change would be made more rapidly than may seem probable at first sight. In fact, the Irish Protestants cannot cling to their estates with the tenacity which, in this respect distinguishes the English race. The man who never lives on his estate, or he who lives surrounded by a population, that, in return for the contempt with which he treats them, regard him with implacable hatred, cannot be bound to his property by very strong moral ties. If he found it to his pecuniary advantage to be freed from it, he would not keep it long. It is probable, therefore, that if land were as easily transferable in Ireland as it is in France, a steady movement would ensue which, little by little, would transfer it from the hands of Protestant proprietors to those of Catholic capitalists.

The Catholics have, during the last century, greatly increased their wealth; the statement of the deposits in the different banks shows that the largest portion of the floating capital of the country belongs to them. They are able, then, to purchase lands, to recover by peaceful means the property wrested from their ancestors. If they do not now, it is because the civil law presents obstacles almost insurmountable.

To remove these, it would suffice to abolish entails and also the right of primogeniture; to permit the partition of inheritances, and to simplify the processes and formalities now required for the sale or division of landed estate. To the British people, indeed, these measures would seem very serious ; they would be regarded by them as expedients almost revolutionary. The present parliament would not readily grant them; but would an Irish parliament be much more disposed to their adoption ? This

is by no means certain; for though these are measures of
vital importance, not a voice in Ireland is raised to
demand them. In all the innumerable speeches of O'Connell, not a single word on the subject is to be found.
Ideas of civil reform are more advanced in Britain than in
Ireland. In Britain a large party already demands such
reforms with·great persistency. One of the leaders of that
party, Mr. Ewart, member of the House of Commons, two
years ago proposed the abolition of primogeniture; in the
discussion that followed that motion, I do not think that a
single Irish orator spoke in its favour. I am more than
inclined to believe that, though O'Connell at times uses
the language of a thorough democrat, he is at heart, as
regards the laws of property, friendly to the aristocratic
system; so that I should be less astonished to see an
Irish parliament adopt violent and revolutionary measures
against the Protestant proprietors, than to see it effect a
complete reform of the civil laws, in the direction of those
principles of equality which the French code has consecrated.

From these considerations, I think I may affirm that as
regards even the amendment of the civil laws, Ireland has
more to hope from the parliament of Great Britain than
from an exclusively national parliament. The opinion
which I have expressed about entails and primogeniture
will astonish, perhaps offend, those who imagine that
the ancient edifice of the British Constitution, mined
on every side, has no other supports than aristocratic
institutions, which cannot be touched without danger of
their falling in ruin. The example of the great reforms
that have been effected during the last twenty years may
well suffice to convince them of their error; but as these

reforms have modified the political and religious laws, rather than the civil laws which maintain the aristocratic organisation of society, their authority may with some reason be denied. I readily make this admission, and I will not use the arguments which these 'reforms might seem to present. But, while I acknowledge the very important place which the aristocracy has held, and still holds, in the British Constitution, I utterly reject the claim of the Irish aristocracy to be regarded as on a similar footing. How can two things so widely different be likened to each other ? What resemblance is there between a nobility which by its intelligence, its talents, its devotedness to the interests of the country, has justly merited its rank at the summit of the British nation, and a class of selfish landowners, alien to the country which they occupy, and hostile to the population which they rule ? The two aristocracies have assuredly no more in common than a sound and vigorous arm has with its fellow which gangrene has blighted.

The improvement of the relations established by law between the proprietors and the tenants, between the minority who possess and the majority who cultivate, is one of the most difficult problems that the legislator can undertake. These relations are in Ireland as bad as possible ; they are, I have already said, the primary cause of the country's distress. No one denies that they need serious reform.

But if the evil is great, the remedies are difficult and still more dangerous. It is to be feared that, in adjusting the relative condition of the proprietors and the tenants, the very right of property may be attacked. Here is a danger against which a legislature, under the control of

the Catholic democracy, would find it hard to defend itself.
I should have little trust, I confess, in the impartiality of
such an assembly when called to decide between the rich
Protestants and the Catholic masses. Let not the protestations of O'Connell be relied upon. He himself would
be powerless to stem the torrent of popular passion,
excited by real suffering and by hatred grown inveterate.
If the Repeal of the Union were carried, if Ireland were
quite free to treat as she thought fit the Protestant landowners, it is almost certain that their rights would be
unscrupulously invaded, and that the principle of property
would be set at nought, however great the danger that
might thence result to the whole social edifice.

These are grave considerations—sufficient, in my view,
to give pause to any sincere person who, moved by a sentiment of unreflecting generosity, looks forward wishfully
to the Repeal of the Union, without, however, desiring that
measure to be the prelude of violent and revolutionary
acts.

Such reflections on the danger of the needful reforms
in the relations of landlord and tenant do not prove that
nothing can be done in this direction. It is, on the contrary, certain that a government enlightened, strong, and
impartial, can by degrees effect great improvements.
During many centuries all the laws have been made in
the exclusive interest of the landowners. Those times of
injustice we have happily left far behind us ; effort is now
needed to obliterate the traces they have left. It is a
laborious task, but one that many statesmen have already
taken in hand, one that I hope will in future be ardently
p ursued. Already a great revolution has been effected in
th e social system of Ireland. It dates from the day when

the Lord Lieutenant, Lord Normanby, in reply to the complaints addressed to him by the proprietors of a county on the disorders of the poorer classes, proclaimed aloud the sacred maxim that "Property has its duties as well as its rights, and the former cannot be violated without injury to the latter." Admirable words, which mark the advent of a new era for Ireland, and announce that the dominion of force is about to give place to the reign of justice and humanity! *

The ministry of Lord Melbourne, by introducing the poor-law into Ireland, by laying down the principle that the landowners are bound to assist the poorer classes in their need, has carried as far as it was permitted the application of Lord Normanby's doctrine. This principle, it is true, has been badly applied. The new poor-law has had but little success, on account as much of the defectiveness of the measures which it necessarily involved, as of the violent and almost factious opposition of the popular party. Nevertheless, whatever may be its immediate results, it will still have the immense merit of establishing

---

* One of the results of our aristocratic system of government is that the figure-head of the vessel is apt to be mistaken—nay, even to mistake itself—for the captain. Though Lord Normanby, in the House of Lords, declared in high official language,—"I *dictated* and directed to be sent a letter,"—there can be no doubt whatever that the memorable sentiment cited by Cavour is due to Mr. Thomas. Drummond, the under-secretary to the Lord Lieutenant of Ireland from 1835 to 1840. The evidence is summed up unanswerably in the Memoir by Mr. Mc.Lennan, pp. 325 - 339. The passage, of which only the first nine words are given *verbatim* in the text, occurs in a letter dated 22nd May, 1838, and addressed to Lord Donoughmore, the Lord Lieutenant of the county of Tipperary. A recent writer, author of "The Pilgrim and the Shrine," 1868, quotes the passage thus :— "Property has its duties as well as its *privileges.*" VoL I., p. 66., B. i., o. 3.—*Translator.*

for the first time in Ireland, that it is at once the right
and the duty of society to impose sacrifices on the richer
classes, in exchange for the benefits secured to them by
the maintenance of social order.

While the right of property is respected, it must still
be possible to do something to improve the relations of
landlord and tenant; such, at least, is the opinion of
intelligent men of all parties.   Mr. Sharman Crawford, a
popular Irish member, had announced in last session of
parliament his intention to bring forward a bill with this
object.   Sir Robert Peel, far from opposing it, declared
that the government was disposed to support every measure
which, without violating the principle of property, should
give to the tenants a greater security of tenure, and
guarantee to them a share of the value added to the land
by their improvements.   The close of the session having
prevented Mr. Crawford from carrying his intention into
effect, the ministry named a commission charged to inquire
into the relations of landowners and tenants in Ireland,
and to prepare a law effecting all the reforms fairly
within the sphere of legislative action.   The just and
honourable character of the man placed at the head of
this commission—the Earl of Devon—is a sure guarantee
of the intentions of the English cabinet.   I do not assert
that it is disposed, as some extreme members desire, to go
so far as to demand an indefinite prolongation of leases,
which would be equivalent to despoiling the proprietors of
all their rights, in order to invest the farmers with them
on a free and invariable payment, but I think that it will
aid all reforms not absolutely incompatible with the spirit
of British legislation.

Would an Irish parliament be better fitted to effect

these reforms ? Surely not. That they may not exceed the limits of reason and of justice, that they may be beneficent without being revolutionary, there are required in the legislator a moderation, a prudence, an impartiality, that cannot be hoped, for a long time at least, in a House of Commons, such as the Repeal of the Union would make it. That assembly, subject to the empire of popular demands, animated by violent passions, would be a bad judge, a partial umpire in the cause pleaded by the tenants against their landlords. There is reason to fear that its sentence would be dictated by a spirit of reaction and of vengeance, which may be as fatal to Ireland in the future, as the spirit of oppression of intolerance has been in the past.

The conscientious examination that we have now made seems to me sufficiently to demonstrate that the advantages which might result from a national legislature are far from counterbalancing the disadvantages and the dangers with which the Repeal of the Union threatens Ireland. I should, therefore, no longer hesitate to declare myself opposed to that measure, and to condemn the sterile agitation of which it is the pretext, if there were not in its favour a last argument which is incessantly put forward, and which, by its plausibility, deceives many impartial persons. This argument is furnished by the habitual absence of very many of the rich landowners. It is by declaiming against the evils of *absenteeism* that O'Connell and his party strive to prove that an Irish parliament, which should restore, by good will or by force, those rich absentees to their country, would be a vast benefit to Ireland.

The argument is serious, and deserves all the more careful consideration on our part, because it has commonly been treated very lightly by politicians on the continent.

I am far from denying the evil consequences of absenteeism in general. On the contrary, I think that they are of two kinds—one moral, the other economic.

It is no slight evil to a country that a considerable portion of the opulent class should be continually absent from it. We cannot too highly estimate the benefits of every kind which result from the habitual residence of landowners on their estates. Of all aristocracies, the most popular is the territorial aristocracy, that which dwells in the midst of the rural population. Such an aristocracy has much more dignity and moral weight than the aristocracy of the court; it is much stronger, more energetic, more generous than the aristocracy of mere finance, which has sprung from commerce and which lives in cities. But what constitutes the true territorial aristocracy, is not merely the possession of a large part of the soil; it is much more the influence which personal relations, continued from generation to generation for centuries, have given to the great proprietors over the population of the country. These relations are rich in happy results for all classes of society, for the highest as for the lowest. They afford to the rich a noble use of their wealth; they secure to the poor greater benevolence and humanity at the hands of the rich. When society rests on solid foundations, when in its constitution there is no abnormal cause of disturbance or of discord, the presence of the proprietors on their estates must have benefical results.

But if, on the contrary, from any cause whatever, between the landed aristocracy and the mass of the people, there exist hostile sentiments and inveterate antipathy, the presence of the former can confer no benefit. To remove the moral consequences of absenteeism, it would not suffice to force the Protestant aristocracy to reside upon their estates. They must first be inspired with more humane and benevolent sentiments towards their Catholic tenants; they must be induced to strive for the improvement of their tenants' condition with the same ardour that they have hitherto shown in retaining them in a state of dependence and oppression. Until this salutary change takes place, as long as the proprietors in general shall be regarded as the oppressors rather than the natural protectors of the country, I do not hesitate to say that absenteeism, whatever may be its economic consequences, will be, in a moral respect, a good more than evil. No pecuniary sacrifices can be compared to the pernicious effects of the presence of a rich class, corrupt and oppressive, in the midst of masses ignorant, passionate, and bitterly hostile.

But, even if the presence of the proprietors on their estates were as beneficial as O'Connell affirms, how could an Irish parliament accomplish this object ? I will go so far as to suppose that by coercive measures, which I do not approve, he forces the Irish proprietors to remain within the island ; but it seems to me utterly impossible for him to compel them to reside on their estates. For this end must be devised a new sort of *lettre de cachet* to condemn the great proprietors, for a part of the year, to *do* philanthropy to the advantage of their tenants. The idea is too absurd to merit the trouble of refutation.

Let us turn to the economic results of absenteeism.

At the outset, I may observe that Ireland is not the

only country that complains of the wrong done to the public wealth by the absence of some of the richest families. England has made the same complaint. During the years that followed the re-establishment of the general peace, public opinion was much disturbed by the danger to the national finances from the increasing emigration to the continent, and more than once there was a question of checking the torrent by fiscal and coercive measures. Experience, however, and the discussions which took place on this subject, having shown that the fear was exaggerated, public opinion was reassured, and declamations against absenteeism dropped into the range of the most vulgar eloquence of mob orators.

The remarkable writings of several economists have contributed much to this result. By a complete analysis of the effects of absenteeism on the production and the consumption of wealth, it has been clearly proved that most frequently it exerts, economically, no injurious effect. The first writer who has treated this subject thoroughly is Mr. Mc.Culloch, the learned editor and commentator of Adam Smith. It is he who first, during an examination that has become famous, maintained before a committee of the House of Lords, that absenteeism was innocent of all the charges brought against it.*   The opinions of Mr.

---

* Mr. Mc.Culloch appends the following note to the chapter on Commerce in his Principles of Political Economy, 2nd edit., Lond., 1830, p. 157, P. i., C. 5 :—"I do not mean, by anything now stated, nor did I ever mean, by anything I have stated on other occasions, to maintain that absenteeism may not be, in several respects, injurious. It would be easy, indeed, to show that both England and Scotland have been largely benefitted by the residence of the great landed proprietors on their estates. No one can doubt that they have been highly instrumental in introducing the manners, and

Mc.Culloch have been generally adopted by economists.
However strange they may at first appear, they are,
within certain limits, perfectly correct. Like almost all
who make discoveries in moral science, however, he has
claimed for his principle a too wide extension. An economist, not less celebrated—Mr. Senior—has subsequently
reduced it within juster limits. Nevertheless, as I think
that these are not yet drawn with perfect exactness, I beg
permission to discuss the question. I shall, I trust, be
pardoned for this short excursion into the domain of
economic science in consideration of the importance of
the subject, and its novelty to some of my readers.

This is Mr. Senior's theory:—" Let us first," he says,
" distinguish between the countries that export primary
materials and those which export manufactured articles.
In the former, the rich man who lives abroad will pay
his expenditure by means of the primary materials of his
country, either directly or indirectly. There is thus no
doubt that a prodigal Irish lord pays his extravagant

---

in diffusing a taste for the conveniences and enjoyments of a more refined
society; and that the improved communications between different places,
the expensive and commodious farm-buildings, and the plantations with
which the country is sheltered and ornamented, are to be, in a great degree,
ascribed to their residence. It may be doubted, however, considering the
circumstances under which most Irish landlords acquired their estates, the
difference between their religious tenets and those of their tenants, the
peculiar tenures under which the latter hold their lands, and the political
condition of the country, whether their residence would have been of any
considerable advantage. But, whatever conclusion may be come to as to
this point, cannot affect what has been stated in the text. The question
really at issue refers merely to the spending of revenue, and has nothing
to do with the improvement of estates; and, notwithstanding all that has
been said to the contrary, I am not yet convinced that absenteeism is, in
this respect, at all injurious."—*Translator.*

H

expenses in London or on the continent by the grain, the pigs, the butter which his lands produce, and which England consumes. If this lord inhabited Ireland, a part at least of those products would be exchanged for Irish labour, and would, consequently, be consumed by the workmen of the country, who would have more bacon to eat, and more butter to give a relish to their potatoes. If, however, this same lord returned home with exclusively English tastes,—if he were attended solely by English servants,—and if he brought from England all that he required, Ireland would gain but little. His grain, his pigs, and his butter would be eaten by the English, or exported to pay for English goods." From this reasoning, of which the truth is obvious, Mr. Senior concludes that absenteeism, in countries which export primary materials, must affect injuriously the national wealth, and tend to depress the rate of wages; and that, consequently, it is desirable for such countries that the idle rich should consume their revenues at home, provided they have not contracted the habit of employing only foreign labour.

" For countries which export manufactured goods," adds Mr. Senior, "the case is different. The rich man, not being able to pay his expenditure by means of the produce of his lands, will exchange it for manufactured goods, which, being exported to the country in which he lives, will pay his debts. This operation is not effected directly. Bankers only in seeming end it by transferrence of paper. It often happens that the products of the country of the absentee, instead of being exported into the country in which he lives, go to pay the debts which he may have contracted with a third country. Nevertheless, through the thousand complications of commercial exchanges, it is easy to reduce the effect of the rich man's expenditure abroad to the operation just explained. Such being the case, his country will have sustained no loss. His income will be exchanged for national labour; only that labour, instead of being consumed by him unproductively at home, will have been employed to pay other services equally unproductive; which he receives from the foreigners among whom he lives."

This second reasoning of Mr. Senior is substantially sound; but he draws from it too wide consequences. If the country in question exported only articles of luxury that did not at all enter into the consumption of the working classes, this able economist would be completely right. As long as the expenditure of the English on the continent is paid with porcelain vases and horses of pure blood, England, far from losing, rather gains. The expenditure of the absentee, increasing the demand for articles of luxury, encourages the development of those branches of industry which bring the best wages and the highest profits. But if the country exports manufactured articles which the working classes do consume,—cheap stuffs, for example,—I do not understand how a different effect can be assigned to absenteeism from that which it produces in countries that export primary materials.

The rich man, it is true, whether he remain at home or go abroad, will equally spend his income on manufactured articles, as we have said he would on the previous hypothesis. But, in the case of these manufactured articles being of a kind employed by the working classes, it is probable that he would not himself consume them; he would exchange them a second time for services suited to satisfy his refined tastes. It will be objected that the same revenue cannot be consumed twice.   That is true; but it must not be forgotten that if the rich man's income goes to pay the service of all those whom he employs, viz., his gamekeeper, grooms, tailor, &c., this kind of consumption, though unproductive from the economic point of view, nevertheless enables his countrymen, who are thus paid, to procure for their own use articles of first necessity which, in the case of the absence of the rich man, would have been exported.

Absenteeism, in these circumstances, does not create a new demand abroad for manufactured articles.   It only displaces it.   It was the servants, the workmen, the tradesmen of the country of the absentee who demanded them ; it is now the servants, the workmen, the tradesmen whom he employs abroad who will profit by them.

In order to throw grave doubts on the theory of Mr. Senior, it is enough to inquire if it is possible for absenteeism to have a different effect on a country which exports oxen, and on that which should export only candles made from the tallow of those same animals.   In one case as in the other, the exportation lessens the quantity of different articles which constitute the real wages of the working classes ; and, consequently, it must tend to lower wages.

If we apply these principles to Ireland, we shall be forced to acknowledge that absenteeism tends to her impoverishment; for that country is one of those that export almost exclusively primary materials, or manufactured articles suitable for the consumption of the lower classes.

It cannot, then, be doubted that an Irish parliament would do a most useful thing if it could retain in Ireland all the rich proprietors who live abroad. But how could this end be attained? Could it be solely by indirect means, by rendering a residence in Dublin as interesting as is now a residence in London? I am very doubtful of the success. It is difficult to change the habits and to modify the tastes of the richer classes. The attraction which will draw them to England, even after the Repeal of the Union, will continue to be more powerful than all the seductions which life in Dublin will be able to offer.

Political interest cannot be much reckoned on as a means of retaining in Ireland the absentee proprietors. They almost all belong to the extreme Tory party; they would lose all influence in an Irish parliament. They would always be in a small minority in the House of Commons, and, as the House of Lords would become insignificant, I do not think that they would be eager to attend, or that they would assiduously perform their legislative functions.

But, it will be said, if the great proprietors, indifferent to the benefits of national independence, persist in living at a distance from their country, coercive means will be employed. This is more easily said than done. I do not suppose that the recipe will be applied which the Emperor of Russia employs to force the nobility to return to the empire—sequestration of their revenues, and even confiscation of their estates. This course would be too violent, too much opposed to the manners, the ideas of our age; no one, except a few pothouse demagogues, would dare to advise it. A tax, then, as a last resource, must be levied on the income of the absentees. This measure, which at the first glance seems simple, would be of very difficult application, perhaps even impossible.

How, indeed, could the absence of any one be established? Would absence during a few months suffice to subject the offender to the tax? Would the whole family be required to stay in Ireland, or its head only? Moreover, what kind of establishment will the rich be required to maintain in their own country? The mere mention of such questions is enough to show that it is almost impossible to answer them. Without instituting a series of inquisitorial and vexatious measures, it will be impossible to impose a tax which will not be universally evaded. It is impossible not to permit temporary absence; and how shall it be limited? Railways and steamboats, which have brought Dublin within twenty-four hours of London,* will enable the rich Irishman, who with his family lives in London, to present himself in Ireland as often as shall be necessary to escape the tax. I repeat that, without adopting an odious system, opposed to all our ideas, to all principles of justice, coercive means for compelling the great Irish nobles to stay at home will be completely vain.

There is, besides, a grave consideration which is commonly lost sight of, but which alone may suffice to dispel the hope of causing absentees to return. It is usually forgotten that the greatest part of the land possessed by non-resident owners belongs to Englishmen, to peers of Great Britain, to powerful corporations. No one can be expected to renounce his quality of Englishman in order to inhabit Ireland. An exceptional measure, accordingly, would be needful to subject such persons to the tax on absentees. This would be in truth a first step in spolia-

---

* Now less than twelve. 1868.—*Translator.*

tion, one to which corporations and other landowners would not readily submit. They would invoke the support of their government, of Britain, and assuredly it would not be withheld. What would happen then? A civil war. This would be in Ireland the height of madness; for not only would she have to contend with material forces far superior to her own, but she would have against her moral forces also—justice and right.

It must, then, be acknowledged that absenteeism is an evil, but that the remedies which O'Connell and his party would apply by means of the Repeal of the Union would be an aggravation of it, not a cure.

I think that I have now completed the most important part of the task which I had imposed upon myself, by demonstrating how far the inevitable consequences of the Repeal of the Union are from fulfilling the expectation of those persons who honestly believe that on the success of this measure depends the salvation of Ireland. If the analysis that I have made is not wholly inexact, it may with certainty be predicted that the advantages which would result from it would be more than counterbalanced by the evils and the dangers that it would cause. It is, accordingly, to be deplored that it should have become the sole object, the sole concern of the Irish popular party. But even though I should have erred, and unduly depreciated the possible benefits of a national legislature, ought we to applaud the course which O'Connell and his party have taken, and which almost all Catholic Ireland has, in appearance at least, adopted with so much energy and invincible determination? Assuredly not; for before encouraging Irish patriots in the perilous path that they have chosen, we must know, not only if the end they seek is legitimate, but further, if it is not beset with insurmountable obstacles, and if it is reasonable to hope that they will succeed, whether by conviction or by force, in breaking the bond which unites them to Great Britain. Now, this is what no men of good sense, after a few moments' reflection, can admit.

How, indeed, could the Repeal of the Union be effected? By legal means? But for this result the consent of parliament must be obtained; and this the immense majority will always be unanimous in refusing. By force? By the fear which Ireland may flatter herself by fancying that she inspires? But who can suppose that Britain would retreat before the menacing attitude of the forces which O'Connell has organised? Those who think so wholly misunderstand the character of the British people, and the principles which guide its government. They are not, it is true, a quickly sensitive people. They act with as much prudence as firmness: when an absolute necessity makes itself felt, they can yield, at the sacrifice even of their vanity and their pride; but when the real interests of the national power, the principles of the national existence, are at stake, they are the most determined people that ever existed, and capable of the most gigantic, the most persevering efforts.

The Repeal of the Union is rightly regarded in Britain, by all parties, as a question of life or death; all, with equal energy, have declared against the separation of the two kingdoms. Though divided in opinion as to the best means of governing that country, and restoring it to tranquillity, the British people are unanimous as to the necessity of maintaining, by all possible means, the incorporation of Ireland with Great Britain. Let it be remembered that

the gentlest, the most humane, the most liberal, the most
sincere member of the Whig party—Lord Spencer—when
he was minister, declared without hesitation that, rather
than consent to the Repeal of the Union, he would advise
parliament to maintain a war of extermination; and, there-
after, let it be judged if it is probable that any British
cabinet whatsoever, supported by the entire nation, would
ever yield to the menaces of O'Connell.

Some persons, deceived by a false historical analogy,
invoke the example of what happened in 1829, when the
Catholics were emancipated, to prove that it is not impossible to wrest from fear important concessions, long refused
to entreaties.   The comparison is inadmissible.   In 1829,
the Irish contended for a cause the justice of which was
evident; and they had on their side, if not a majority of
the British people, at least a very imposing minority, in
whose ranks were reckoned not merely the whole Whig
party, but even the most eminent and most enlightened
Tories.   The Duke of Wellington did not give way merely
on account of the threatening attitude of the Catholic
Association; he yielded, because, as a skilful leader, he
saw that his army was not resolved to follow him into a
deadly strife.   He wielded, it is true, the majority in both
chambers, and he could, with an effort, have caused the
defeat of any direct motion in favour of the Catholics;
but it would have been difficult and almost impossible for
him to obtain from the House of Commons the extraordinary powers needful forcibly to suppress the formidable
agitation which O'Connell had organised.

The circumstances are now very different.   In Great
Britain, both in parliament and in the country, there
is unanimity against the Repeal of the Union.   This

measure is rejected equally by the fanatical partisans of all existing things, and by the most ardent friends of progress. This universal agreement is not due wholly to the mere sentiment of the national interest; it must, in great part, be ascribed to the loyal and honest conviction which regards the disruption of the bond that unites the British islands as a hateful and criminal enterprise. The ministry, whatever it may be, will always find parliament prepared to arm it with all the necessary legal powers, and to place at its disposal sufficient material resources to maintain in Ireland the existing legal order, whether by means of the laws or by force.

The systematic legal agitation, such as O'Connell has conducted, is, therefore, doomed to be and to continue barren. The promises, the boasts, of the Liberator may, in this respect, continue to maintain illusions in the minds of the Irish Catholics; but these illusions will, sooner or later, be dispelled, and the popular party will, in the end, demand from its leader an account of the results of so great efforts, so great sacrifices. What will, then, be the course of the great man whose influence on the destinies of Ireland is so powerful? Abandoning the issueless path which he has entered, will he resort to the final argument of oppressed nations, to insurrection, to civil war? I cannot believe it. O'Connell is too skilful, too enlightened; he has too much good sense to engage seriously in a death-struggle with Great Britain. The chances would be too unequal. Some persons are, I know, of a contrary opinion; they believe that on the day when O'Connell shall unfurl the banner of the Independence of Ireland, and appeal to the national forces, an irresistible popular movement will ensue. They say: In this age it is impossible to keep down by force eight millions of men resolved to conquer or to die. Here again is an illusion which will quickly be removed by a careful study of the elements that compose the population of the British empire.

In the first place, let it be remembered that Ireland is not unanimous ; that in that country there is a numerous and powerful class, bound by all their interests to .the Union, and to whom the question of Repeal is a question of life or death. The Protestants are indeed only a small numerical majority ; but they are strong by their wealth, by their energy, and by their organisation. At the first cry of insurrection they would rise in mass, and with the aid of the regular troops, they would unhesitatingly attack the assemblages of Catholics in revolt.

In respect of popular warfare the people of the British Isles differs essentially from the French people. In France, the use of arms is general ; the military spirit pervades all classes of society ; it is even stronger in the lower than in the upper classes. The conscription has taught the great majority of the nation how to fight ; there is not a village in which a company or a platoon cannot be organised in a day. Combats in the streets are, consequently, dangerous in France ; the people more than once have been victorious. In Ireland, as in Britain, on the contrary, the people have not military instincts or military habits. The army is to them something foreign. The people furnish it with soldiers, indeed ; but these, once enrolled, return no more into the ranks of the people. The armed force produces a magical effect upon the masses. Small detachments have often sufficed to disperse groups, seemingly the most threatening. However the courage of the Irish soldiers may be over-rated, and in spite of O'Connell's boasts, no one acquainted with Ireland can, for a moment, believe that the popular masses would be able to oppose a serious resistance to regular troops.

The middle and the upper classes constitute the living strength of the British nation. They are much more energetic than the similar classes on the continent. No revolution, no attempt at insurrection is possible if the majority of the persons composing these do not declare against the government. Now nothing is less probable in Ireland. If civil war broke out, we should see on one side numerous and confused masses of undisciplined peasants, commanded by a small number of Catholics belonging to the upper ranks of society; and, on the other side, the upper and the middle classes supported by all the force at the disposal of the government. The contest would, in truth, be too unequal. The popular party, by resorting to violence, would rush upon certain ruin.

There is no chance, not the slightest, that could turn the scale in favour of the Irish insurrection, or make the balance even. There might be an unsuccessful foreign war that would exhaust the strength of Britain. In that case, I confess, the Irish might successfully attempt an insurrection. But can this extreme case enter into the calculations of reasonable men ? Can we approve a party that founds its chances of success on the humiliation of its country ?* No ! a thousand times no. Repeal obtained

---

* But, unhappily, though not quite unreasonably, too many Irishmen refuse to recognise Britain as *their* country. "Britain," they say, "is not our friend; nor British law." England AND Scotland *are* Great Britain; but we say Great Britain AND Ireland.—*Translator.*

at the price of the humiliation of Britain would cost humanity too dear. No one of good faith can desire it at this price.

But, in fine, I shall be asked what conclusion is to be drawn from all the reasoning by which I have endeavoured to ascertain the present state of the questions relating to the condition of Ireland. In the first place, I have a firm conviction that Repeal will not be effected. But I shall next, perhaps, be asked, what then will happen? What will be the issue of the present crisis, and what will be the *dénouement* of the drama in which O'Connell plays so extraordinary a part? I cannot, and I will not, expatiate in the field of conjectures and predictions. I have already said, it is permitted to no one to foresee the mysteries of the future. The social horizon is closely limited; men of the greatest genius have striven in vain to cross its bounds. Nevertheless, without hazarding any rash hypothesis, I think I may end this article—already too long—by affirming that it is probable the present ministry and those which shall follow it will continue to apply to Ireland the system of amelioration and of reform which Lord Melbourne was the first to adopt on a broad basis. The insults, the violence of O'Connell and his followers, so long as he shall not transgress legality, will not arrest the march of the British government. Long accustomed to the extreme consequences of political liberty, the government is not sensitive or timid. It does not allow itself to be moved either by vain threats, or by the fear of seeming to yield through weakness, when the time for concession has come. It will then pursue the work of the regeneration of Ireland. Its march will be measured and prudent; perhaps even it will be exceedingly slow; but it will be constant, and nothing will make it turn back. In support of what I have said, I will only cite the moderate, liberal, generous conduct of the cabinet of Sir Robert Peel towards Canada.

What it did for that distant colony it will do for Ireland. After having conquered Canada by force of arms, it has chosen to conciliate it by large concessions. In like manner, if it gain over O'Connell a legal victory, and so, too, if it be obliged to repress by material force bolder attempts, it will not the less endeavour to give to the demands of the Irish all the satisfaction that is compatible with the interests of Great Britain and with the requirements of its party.

What, then, will be the final result of these progressive and moderate reforms? Will they succeed in radically curing the wounds of Ireland, and in completely fusing the sentiments and the interests of that country with those of Britain? These are grave questions which only the future can resolve. I hope, and I ardently desire, that the solution will be favourable to that Ireland which is so worthy of interest, and which inspires so deep attachment. May the real progress which the efforts of honest men of all parties, aided by time, must accomplish, compensate her for the loss of those brilliant dreams of national independence that she can never realise!

A. Ireland and Co., Printers, Pall Mall, Manchester.

www.ingramcontent.com/pod-product-compliance
Lightning Source LLC
Chambersburg PA
CBHW030625270326
41927CB00007B/1308